To my most precious treasure, my Beautiful Wife Jennifer Margaret Martha[2] D'Eathe.

Copyright © 2021

CONTENTS

THE MEANING AND BASICS OF BANSHEES

The banshee is perhaps connected with ancestral or house spirits. The Wild Huntsman, the Gabriel hounds, the Seven Whistlers & etc., are traceable to some actual phenomenon. But the great mass of Irish goblindom cannot now be traced back to savage or barbarous analogues. In Ireland, legends of the banshee belong more particularly to certain families in whose records periodic visits from the spirit are chronicled.

The Irish banshee is held to be the distinction only of families of pure Milesian descent. Even Inspector Declan O'Donoghue was there, and the town Garda commisioner and, in various costumes of nightwear, Fred, the Quincy sisters and Gladys Slevin, who'd let out a banshee scream that woke everyone but poor Edith Shipton, who'd never wake again.

In a country like Ireland, that is portrayed by an arrestive and uncontrollably excellent landscape, it isn't at all astounding to discover something in the idea of an apparition blending with the overall climate and environmental factors, and that something, clearly so characteristic to Ireland, is the Banshee.

The name Banshee is by all accounts a withdrawal of the Irish Bean Sidhe, which is deciphered by certain authors regarding the matter "A Woman of the Faire Race," while by different essayists it is said to mean "The Lady of Death," "The Woman of Sorrow," "The Spirit of the Air," and "The Woman of the Barrow." In all cases this is a supernatural race or species, connected to nature with power and control over human, more directly, over Irish people.

It is stringently a family phantom, and most specialists concur that it just frequents groups of antiquated Irish heredity. Mr Michael, for example, comments (in the section on Banshees in his "Irish Wonders"): "The Banshee goes to just the old families, and however their relatives, through hardship, might be brought down from high domain to positions of worker ranchers, she never leaves nor fails to remember them till the last part has been accumulated to his dads in the churchyard."

An essayist in the Journal of the Cork Historical and Archeological Society cites a concentrate from a work named "Kerry Records," in which the accompanying entry, identifying with an elegiac sonnet composed by Pierse Ferreter on Maurice Fitzgerald, happens: "Aina, the Banshee who never moaned for any families who were not of Milesian blood, except for the Geraldine's, who turned out to be 'more Irish than the actual Irish'; it is just 'blood' that can have a Banshee. Money managers these days have something comparable to 'blood'— they have 'minds and metal,' by which they can rival and go into the most seasoned families in Britain and Ireland. Nothing, be that as it may, in an Irishman's assessment, can supplant 'nobility.'"

Sir John, as well, underlines this point and is significantly more explicit and subjective. He limits the Banshee to groups of unadulterated Milesian stock, and proclaims it is never to be discovered connected to the relatives of the incalculable English and Scotch pilgrims who have, every once in a while, relocated to Ireland; nor even to the relatives of the Norman travelers who went with Strongbow to the Green Isle in the twelfth century.

Woman Wilde goes to the next outrageous and permits impressive scope. She insists that the Banshee connects itself not exclusively to specific groups of memorable heredity, yet in addition to people talented with melody and music. For my part, I am slanted to embrace a center course; I don't accept that the Banshee would be deflected from frequenting a group of chronicled distinction and Milesian drop—like the O'Neill's or O'Donnell's—basically because in that family was an infrequent strain of Saxon or Norman blood, yet, then again, I don't figure the Banshee could at any point frequent a family that was not initially at any rate Celtic Irish—such, for example, as the Fitz-Williams or Fitz-Warrens—albeit in that family there may turn out to be occasional implantations of Milesian blood.

I deviate, in all, with Lady Wilde's hypothesis that, infrequently, the Banshee frequents an individual who is amazingly poetical and melodic, essentially because he turns out to be along these lines skilled. As I would see it, to be spooky by the Banshee one should have a place with an Irish family that is, in any event, 1,000 years of age; where it not really, we ought to without a doubt discover the Banshee frequenting sure of the melodic and poetical prodigies of each race everywhere on the world—dark and yellow, maybe, not exactly white—which unquestionably isn't the situation.

The Banshee, in any case, as Mr. Michael says, does, now and again, travel. It voyages when, and just when, it goes with abroad perhaps the eldest of the Irish families; else it stays in Ireland, where, inferable from the way that there are not many of the truly old Irish families left, its exhibits are getting increasingly uncommon.

It might, maybe, be said that in Dublin, Cork, and other of the Irish towns one may, in any case, go over a reasonable level of O's and Macs, that, without a doubt, is valid, at the same time, simultaneously, it should be borne as a primula concern that these prefixes don't constantly indicate the genuine Irishman, since numerous families yclept Thompson, Walker, and Smith, just on the strength of having lived in Ireland for a few ages, have embraced an Irish—and now and again, even, a Celtic Irish name, depending upon their insight into a couple of Celtic words got from books. Or from going to a portion of the various classes presently being held in essentially every one of the large towns, and which are directed by instructors who are additionally, generally, only pseudo-Irish—to offer tone to their case. Such a misrepresentation, nonetheless, doesn't mislead the individuals who are truly Irish, neither does it delude the Banshee, and the last mentioned, I am very certain, could never be convinced to follow the fortunes of any Anglo-Saxon, or Scotch, Dick, Tom, or Harry, regardless of how cunning and persuading their cover may be.

By and by, at that point, the Banshee limits itself exclusively to groups of genuine antiquated Irish drop. Concerning its source, notwithstanding self-assertive affirmations made by specific individuals, none of whom, coincidentally, are of Irish extraction—that nobody knows. In actuality the Banshee has various causes, for there isn't one Banshee in particular—as such countless individuals assume—yet many: every faction having its very own Banshee.

The O'Donnell Banshee, for instance, in other words, the Banshee joined to our part of the group, and to which I can affirm from individual experience, is, I accept, totally different in appearance, and in its way of spreading the word about itself, from the Banshee of the Reardon's, as depicted by Mr. Michael; while the Banshee of a specific part of the O'Flaherty's, as indicated by this equivalent power, contrasts basically from that of a part of the O'Neill's. Mr. Michael says the Banshee "is an immaterial soul, that of one who, throughout everyday life, was unequivocally joined to the family, or who had valid justification to abhor every one of its individuals." This definition may apply now and again, however it unquestionably doesn't make a difference on the whole, and it is silly to be stubborn regarding a matter, concerning which it is very difficult to acquire a lot of data. And no more, Mr. Michael can just talk with the sureness of the relatively couple of instances of Banshees that have gone under his perception; there are, I think, scores of which he has never at any point heard. I, when all is said and done, know about a few Banshee hauntings in which the ghost positively can't be that of any individual from humanity;

its highlights and extents negative such a chance, and I ought to have no dithering in confirming that, in these cases, the apparition is the thing that is regularly known as an essential, or what I have named in past of my works, a nutarian, that is a soul that has never occupied any material body, and which has a place with animal categories completely unmistakable from man.

Then again, a few instances of Banshee hauntings I have run over without a doubt concede the chance of the ghost being that of a lady having a place with humankind, yet to an old and since a long time ago outdated part of it; while a couple, in particular, permit of the likelihood of the apparition being that of a lady, additionally human, yet having a place with an especially later date.

Unquestionably, as Mr. Michael expressed, Banshees might be isolated into two principal classes, the Friendly Banshees and the Hateful Banshees; the previous showing distress on their appearance, and the last mentioned, celebration. However, these classes can do practically unending sub-division; the lone component they have in like manner being a dubious something that emphatically recommends the ladylike sex. By and large the reason for the hauntings must involve guess. Fondness or wrongdoing may represent a few, be that as it may, for the inception of others, I trust one should glance in a very surprising area. For example, one may, maybe, see some arrangement in divination and black magic, since there should be numerous families, who, in past days, fiddled with those pursuits, that are presently Banshee ridden.

Or then again, allowed there is a trace of validity in the hypothesis of Atlantis, the hypothesis that an entire mainland was lowered attributable to the mischievousness of its occupants, who were all pretty much adepts in magic—the eldest of the Irish, the alleged Milesian families who are known to have drilled magic, likely could be indistinguishable with the overcomers of that extraordinary calamity, and have carried with them to the Green Island spirits which have adhered to their relatives from that point onward.

I figure one may excuse Mr. C. W. Leadbeater's and other essayists' (of a similar would-be definitive request) statement that family apparitions might be either an idea structure or a bizarrely clear impression in the astral light, as silly. Mystics and others, who aimlessly veneration highfalutin style, anyway, void it could be, may be happy with such a clarification, yet not so the individuals who have had a genuine encounter with the apparition being referred to.

Whatever else the Banshee may, or may not be, it is assuredly an inhabitant of a world very particular from our own; it is, furthermore, a being that has prophetic forces (which would not be the situation if it were a simple idea structure or impression), and it is in no way, shape or form a simple robot or advance technology.

A few Banshees address excellent ladies—ladies with long, rich braids, both of raven dark, or shined copper, or splendid gold, and whose star-like eyes, loaded with delicate pity, are either dim and mournful, or of the most wonderful blue or dim; a few, once more, are haggish, wild, tousled looking animals, whose appearance proposes the most extreme dirtiness, revoltingness, and despair; while a couple, luckily, I think, a couple, appear as something that is completely underhanded, and appalling, and alarming in the limit.

When in doubt, nonetheless, the Banshee isn't seen, it is just heard, and it declares its approach in an assortment of ways; now and again by moaning, by howling, and at times by articulating the most blood-souring of shouts, which I can compare to the shouts a lady may make on the off chance that she was being done to death in an extremely barbarous and fierce way. Once in a while I have known about Banshees applauding and tapping and scratching at dividers and window-sheets, and, not inconsistently, I have known about them flagging their appearance by dynamite crashes and pounds. Additionally, I have met with the Banshee that laughs—a low, short, yet horrendously expressive laugh, that establishes multiple times more connection with the psyche of the listener than some other spooky sound he has heard, and which no pass of time is ever ready to destroy from his memory.

I most definitely, have heard the sound, and as I stay here writing these lines, I extravagant I can hear it once more—a Satanic laugh, a laugh brimming with joke, as though made by one who was in the full information on coming occasions, of occasions that would introduce an incredibly upsetting shock. Furthermore, for my situation, the horrendous shock came. I have consistently been an adherent to a soul world—in the obscure—however, had I been doubtful beforehand, in the wake of hearing that laugh, I am very certain I ought to have been changed over. In closing this part, I should allude by and by to Mr. Michael, who, in his "Irish Wonders," records an entirely astounding case of various Banshees showing themselves all the while. He says that the exhibits happened before the passing of an individual from the Galway O'Flaherty's "a few years prior." The bound one, he states, was a woman of the strangest devotion, who, however sick at that point, was not an idea to be truly sick. She improved that few of her associates went to her space to breathe life into her recovery, and it was the point at which they were there, all talking together joyfully, that singing was abruptly heard, obviously outside the window. They tuned in, and could unmistakably hear an ensemble of extremely sweet voices singing some phenomenally sad air, which made them turn pale and take a gander at each other fearfully, for they all felt naturally it was a chorale of Banshees. Nor were them deduces off base, for the patient suddenly created pleurisy, and passed on inside a couple of days, a similar ensemble of soul voices being again heard right now of actual disintegration.

Be that as it may, as Mr. Michael expresses, the doomed woman was of a particular virtue, which without a doubt clarifies the motivation behind why, in my investigates, I have never gone over an equal case.

SOME CHRONICLED BANSHEES

Among the most famous instances of Banshee frequenting both distributed and unpublished is that related by Ann, Lady Fanshawe, in her Memoirs. It appears to be that Lady Fanshawe encountered this unpleasant being when on a visit to Lady Honora O'Brien, the girl of Henry, fifth Earl of Thomond, who was at that point, without a doubt, living at the old palace of Lemonish, close to Lake Antiquing, around thirty miles north-west of Limerick. Resigning to rest to some degree promptly the primula evening of her visit there, she was stirred at around one o'clock by the sound of a voice, and, drawing to the side the hangings of the bed, she saw, glancing in through the window at her, the substance of a lady. The twilight being solid and completely focused on it, she could see each element with frightening uniqueness; and yet her consideration was bolted on the remarkable paleness of the cheeks and the extraordinary redness of the hair. At that point, to cite her own words, the nebulous vision "space noisy, and in a tone, I never heard, threefold 'Atone,' and afterwards with a moan, more like breeze than breath, she disappeared, and to me, her body looked more like a thick cloud than substance.

"I was such a lot of alarmed that my hair remained on end, and my night garments tumbled off. I pulled and squeezed your dad, who never awaked during this problem I was in, yet finally was highly astounded to discover me in this fear, and more when I related the story and showed him the window opened; however, he engaged me with telling the amount more these phantoms were regular in that country than in England."

The next morning Lady Honora, who didn't seem to have been to bed, educated Lady Fanshawe that a cousin of hers had kicked the bucket in the house at around two AM; and communicated an expectation that

Lady Fanshawe had not been exposed to any aggravations.

"At the point when any bite the dust of this family," she said via clarification, "there is the state of a lady shows up in this window consistently until they are dead."

She proceeded to add that the spirit was accepted to be that of a lady who, hundreds of years prior, had been allured by the proprietor of the palace and killed, her body being covered under the window of the room in which Lady Fanshawe had rested.

However, she commented, via a statement of regret, "I considered not it when I stopped you here."

Another notable instance of the Banshee is that identifying with the O'Flaherty's of Galway, reference being put forth to the defence by Mr. Michael in his work named "Irish Wonders." In the times of a lot between-group battling in Ireland when the O'Neill's oftentimes left on campaigns against their substitute companions and adversaries the O'Donnell's and the O'Rourke set out on comparable campaigns against the O'Donovan's. It so happened that one night the head of the O'Flaherty's, exhibited in all the brightness of another suit of reinforcement, and feeling more than generally lively and fit, walked out of his palace at the top of a various body of his retainers, who were all, similar to their boss, feeling great, and talking and singing merrily. They had not continued far, in any case, when an unexpected and very mysterious quietness resulted in a quiet that was suddenly broken by a progression of anguishing shouts, that appeared to come from simply over their heads. In a flash, everybody was calmed and normally turned upward, hoping to see something that would clarify the uncommon and alarming aggravation; nothing, notwithstanding, was to be seen, only an immense territory of a cloudless sky, countless glimmering stars, and the moon which was sparkling forward in all the peaceful magnificence of its peak. However, regardless of the way that nothing was obvious, everybody felt a presence that was without a moment's delay tragic and odd, and which everyone naturally knew was the Banshee, the orderly soul of the O'Flaherty's, come to caution them of some moving toward disaster.

The following evening, when the tribal leader and his devotees were again sallying forward, the same thing occurred, however, from that point onward, nothing of a comparable sort happened for about a month. At that point, the spouse of the O'Flaherty, during the shortfall of her significant other on one of these rummaging campaigns, had an encounter. She had hit the hay one evening and was fretfully throwing about, for, attempt how she would, she was unable to rest, when she was unexpectedly panicked by a progression of the most terrible yells, coming, obviously, from just underneath her window, and which seemed like the calls of some lady in the direst difficulty or torment. She looked, yet as she naturally felt would be the situation, she could see nobody. She at that point realized that she had heard the Banshee, and on the morrow, her premonitions were quite completely figured out. With a piece of unfortunate information on its significance, she saw a parade, bearing in its middle a coffin, gradually and dismally wending its way towards the palace; and she didn't need to be informed that the scavenging party had returned and that the enduring champions had carried back with them the dormant and ruined body of her better half.

The Keneally Banshee outfits one more case of this incredibly entrancing and, up to the present, completely enigmatical kind of frequent. Dr Keneally, the notable Irish artist and creator, dwelled in his previous years in an uncontrollably heartfelt and beautiful piece of Ireland. Among his siblings was one, a simple kid, whose sweet and delicate nature delivered him adored by all, and it involved the most unreasonable despondency to the whole family, and, without a doubt, the entire area, when this kid fell into a decrease and his life was given up all hope of by the doctors. As time went on, he became more vulnerable and more fragile, until the second finally showed up, when clearly, he couldn't in any way, shape or form endure another 24 hours.

At about early afternoon, the room where the patient lay was overwhelmed with a surge of daylight, which came pouring through the windows from the cloudless span of sky overhead. The climate, in reality, was dazzling to such an extent that it appeared to be practically mind-blowing that passing could be floating so close to the house. Individually, members from the family took into the chamber to take what everyone felt might be a last gander at the debilitated kid, while he was as yet alive. By and by the specialist showed up, and, as they were all examining in quieted tones the state of the poor squandered and destined youngster, they, the whole gang heard somebody singing, obviously in the grounds, quickly underneath the window. The voice appeared to be that of a lady, however not a lady of this world. It was supernaturally delicate and sweet and accused of a pity and distress that no natural being might have depicted, and now uproarious, and now quieted, it proceeded for certain minutes, and afterwards appeared to fade away bit by bit, similar to the wave of a wavelet on some brilliant, sun-kissed strand, or the murmuring of the breeze, as it tenderly stirs its way through many a field of yellow, gesturing corn.

"What a great voice!" one of the audience members shouted. "I've heard nothing to rise to it."

"Likely not," another person murmured, "it's the Banshee!"

Thus, excited were they all by the singing, that it was just when the last note of the mournful tune had very stopped, that they became mindful that their cherished patient, unseen by them, had dropped. It appeared as though the kid's spirit, with the last murmuring notes of the requiem, had joined the delightful, feeling sorry for Banshee, to be accompanied by it into the domains of the all-unfortunate, all-restless Unknown. Dr Keneally has honoured this occasion in one of his sonnets.

The tale of another frequenting by the cordial Banshee is told in Kerry, regarding a specific family that used to live there. As per my wellspring of data the family comprised of a man (a respectable man rancher), his significant other, their child, Terence, and a little girl, Norah.

Norah, an Irish stunner of the dim kind, had dark hair and blue eyes; and having various admirers, supported none of them even a specific Michael Lernaean.

Presently Michael didn't stand very well in the graces of both of Norah's folks, however, Terence preferred him, and he was presumed to be rich—in other words, rich for that piece of Ireland. In like manner, he was welcomed pretty unreservedly to the homestead, and no impediments were set in his direction. He was given over a decent measure of support.

Finally, as had been for quite some time expected, he proposed and Norah acknowledged him; yet no sooner was her pledge plighted than the two of them heard, simply over their heads, a low, hopeless cry, starting at a lady in the best misery and torment.

Even though they were tremendously frightened at that point, being positive that the sounds continued from no person, neither of them appears to have respected the marvel looking like an admonition, and both proceeded with their adoration making as though the occurrence had never happened. Half a month later, notwithstanding, Norah saw an unexpected change in her sweetheart; he was colder and more far off, and, while he was with her, she constantly discovered him engrossed. Finally, the blow fell. He neglected to introduce himself at the house one evening, however, he was normal obviously, and, as no clarification was impending the next morning, nor on any of the succeeding days, requests were made by the guardians, which inspired the way that he had become connected with to another young lady and that the young lady's house was nevertheless a couple of moments' strolls from the ranch.

This demonstrated a lot for Norah; albeit, clearly, neither bizarrely touchy nor especially profoundly hung, she became sick, and instantly a while later kicked the bucket of a messed-up heart. It was not until the prior night she passed on, nonetheless, that the Banshee paid her a subsequent visit. She was lying on a lounge chair in the parlour of the farmhouse, with her mom sitting alongside her, when a commotion was heard that seemed as though leaves beating tenderly against the window-outlines, and, straightforwardly a while later, came the sound of singing, noisy, and loaded with exceptional distress and empathy; and clearly, that of a lady.

"'Tis' the Banshee," the mother murmured, quickly crossing herself, and, simultaneously, sobbing uncontrollably.

"The Banshee," Norah rehashed. "Sure, I hear only that tapping at the window and the breeze which appears to be out of nowhere to have risen."

Be that as it may, the mother made no reaction. She just sat with her face covered in her grasp, wailing harshly and mumbling to herself, "Banshee! Banshee!"

As of now, the singing had stopped, the elderly person got up and dried her tears. Her tension, be that as it may, was not eased; all during that time she could, in any case, be heard, sometimes, crying unobtrusively and murmuring to herself "Taws the Banshee! Banshee!"; and in the first part of the day Norah, unexpectedly becoming alarmingly badly, died before clinical help could be gathered.

An instance of Banshee frequenting that is to some degree strangely despicable was once identified with me regarding a Dublin part of the once amazing tribe of McGrath. It occurred in the fifties, and the family, comprising of a youthful widow and two youngsters, Isa and David, around then involved an old, meandering aimlessly house, not five minutes' stroll from Stephen's Green. Isa appears to have been the mother's top pick—she was without a doubt an exceptionally beautiful and appealing kid—and David, perhaps under his articulated resemblance to his dad, with whom it was a loosely held bit of information that Mrs. McGrath had never got on at all well, to have gotten preferably more over something reasonable of admonishing. This, obviously, could conceivably have been valid. Surely, he was left particularly to himself, and, in isolation, in a major, void room at the highest point of the house, had to delight himself as he best could. Incidentally, one of the workers, enlivened by an individual inclination—for the part of workers back then, particularly when serving under such extreme and demanding escorts as Mrs. McGrath, was none excessively ruddy—used to glance in to perceive how he was getting on and present to him a toy, purchased out of her pitiful reserve funds; and, when once in a while, Isa, clad in some exorbitant new dress, just popped her head in at the entryway, either to present to him some message from her mom or only to call out "Hello!" Otherwise, he saw nobody, at any rate, having a place with this world; he just saw, he avowed, on occasion, weird-looking individuals who essentially stood and gazed at him without talking, individuals who the workers—young ladies from

Limerick and the west nation—guaranteed him were either pixies or phantoms.

One day Isa, who had been sent higher up to advise David to go to his room to clean himself, as he was needed quickly in the drawing-room, discovered him in an incredible condition of energy.

"I've seen a particularly delightful woman," he shouted, "and she wasn't somewhat cross. She came and remained by the window and looked as though she needed to play with me, just I do not ask her. Do you figure she will return once more?"

"How might I tell? I expect you've been dreaming obviously," Isa chuckled. "How was she?"

"Gracious, tall. A lot taller than mother," David answered, "with incredibly, blue eyes and sort of ruddy gold hair that wasn't completely botched on her head, yet was hanging in twists on her shoulders. She had white hands which were fastened before her and a radiant green dress. I didn't see her come or go, yet she was here for quite a while, every ten minutes."

"It's another of your likes, David," Isa chuckled once more. "In any case, go along, make scurry, or mother will be irate."

A couple of moments later, David, looking timid and off-kilter, was in the next room being acquainted with an honourable man what his identity was, educated, was his future daddy.

David appears to have taken a solid abhorrence to him from the absolute first, and to have anticipated in the coming collusion just a burden and wretchedness for himself. Nor were his fears without establishment, for, straightforwardly after the marriage occurred, he got exposed to the strictest order. Morning and evening the same he was kept hard at his books, and any gradualness or powerlessness to dominate an exercise was treated as inaction and rebuffed as needs to be. The minutes he needed to himself in his dearest nursery currently got rare, for, straightforwardly he had completed his evening planning, he was given his dinner and pressed off to bed.

A couple of workers who had become a close acquaintance with him, incapable to endure the new system, pulled out and left, and there was soon nobody in the house who showed any empathy whatever for the poor desolate kid.

Things went on in this style for certain weeks, and afterwards, a day came when he truly felt it difficult to continue living any more.

He had been by and large overviewing for certain weeks, and this, combined with the way that he was broken in the soul, delivered his assignment of learning a well-nigh inconceivability. It was to no end he argued, notwithstanding; his pleas were just taken for pardons; and, when, in an unguarded second, he let slip a type of reference to heartless treatment, he was immediately blamed for impoliteness by his mom and, at her solicitation, immediately blasted.

The constraint of his affliction had been reached. That evening he was shipped off the bed, obviously, following dinner, and Isa, who ended up passing by his room an hour or so a short time later, was enormously astounded at hearing him occupied with discussion. Peeping cleverly in at the entryway, to discover with whom he was talking, she saw him sitting up in bed, evidently tending to space, or the moonbeams, which, pouring in at the window, fell straightforwardly on him.

"What are you doing?" she asked, "and for what reason would you say you aren't sleeping?"

The second she talked he looked round and, in tones of the biggest frustration, said:

"Goodness, dear, she's no more. You've terrified her away."

"Terrified her away! Isa shouted. "Rests immediately or I'll proceed to bring mamma."

"It was my green woman," David went on, enthusiastically, unreasonably eager to pay any genuine notice to Isa's danger. "My green woman and she revealed to me I ought to be not any more forlorn, that she was coming to get me some an ideal opportunity tonight."

Isa giggled, and, revealing to him not to be so senseless, however, to rest immediately, she rapidly pulled out and went down the stairs to join her folks in the drawing-room.

That evening, at around twelve, Isa was stirred by singing, boisterous and sad singing, in a lady's voice, clearly continuing from the corridor. Significantly frightened she got up, and, on opening her entryway, seen her folks and the workers, all in their night clothing, crouched together on the arrival, tuning in.

"Sure, 'tis the Banshee," the cook finally murmured. "I heard my dad space about it when I was a youngster. She sings, says he, more wonderfully than any terrific woman, however sad like, and just before a demise."

"Before a demise," Isa's mom stammered. "In any case, who will bite the dust here? Because we are all completely stable and well." As she talked the singing stopped, there was a sudden quietness, and all gradually resigned to their rooms.

Nothing further was heard during the evening, however toward the beginning of the day, when breakfast opportunity arrived, there was no David; and a shout being raised and an exhaustive hunt made, he was at last found, suffocated in a reservoir in the rooftop.

THE VINDICTIVE BANSHEE

The Banshees managed in the last part may all be portrayed as thoughtful or amicable Banshees. I will currently present to the peruse a couple of similarly legitimate records of malignant or threatening Banshees. Before doing as such, notwithstanding, I might want to point out the way that, when I was perusing a paper on Banshees before the Irish Literary Society, in Hanover Square, a woman got up and, testing my comment that not all Banshees were indistinguishable, attempted to refute that I was, with the understanding that all Banshees should be miserable and excellent because the Banshee in her family turned out to be pitiful and delightful, a contention, if contention it very well may be called, which, although it is a genuinely regular one, can't be viewed appropriately.

Besides, as I have effectively expressed, there is plentiful proof to show that Banshees are of numerous and different sorts; and that no two have all the earmarks of being by and large indistinguishable or to act in absolutely a similar design.

As per Mr. Michael, the noxious Banshee is constantly "a repulsive witch with appalling, contorted highlights; criticisms are written in each line of her wrinkled face, and her outstretched arms call down curses on the destined individual from the detested race."

Different essayists, as well, would appear to be pretty much to support the possibility that all threatening Banshees are projected in one form and all lovely Banshees in another, while from my very own encounters I should say that Banshees, regardless of whether positive or negative, are similarly just about as individual as any individual from the family they frequent.

It is connected of a specific antiquated Mayo family that ahead of the race once had intercourse with a delightful young lady whom he double-crossed and therefore killed. With her withering breath, the young lady reviled her killer and swore she would frequent him and his forever. A long time moved by; the remorseless double-crosser wedded, and, with the dying of all who knew him in his childhood, he came to be viewed as a model of supreme respectability and integrity. Thus, it was in these conditions that he was sitting one night before a major bursting fire in the lobby of his palace, ostensibly glad enough and encircled by his children and girls, when uproarious yells of jubilee were heard coming, it appeared, from somebody who was remaining on the way near the palace dividers. All hurried out to see what its identity was, however, nobody was there, and the grounds, the extent that the eye could reach, were abandoned.

Later on, in any case, some brief period after the family had resigned to rest, similar demoniacal unsettling influences occurred; a great many rings of wild, pernicious chuckling rang out, trailed by a dissonant groaning and shouting. This time the matured clan leader didn't go with the remainder of the family as they continued looking for the originator of the unsettling influences. Perhaps, in that grating groaning and shouting he liked he could distinguish the voice of the killed young lady; and, potentially, tolerating the sign as a demise notice, he was not amazed on the next day, when he was waylaid out of entryways and fiercely done to death by one of his supporters.

Maybe, the frequenting of this Banshee proceeds, similar marvels happening in any event once to each age of the family, before the passing of one of its individuals. Cheerfully, notwithstanding, the frightful currently doesn't go before a rough passing, and in this regard, however in this regard just, varies from the first.

Another frequenting by this equivalent type of Banshee was brought to my notification the last time I was in Ireland. I turned out to visit a specific relative of mine, at that date dwelling in Black Rock, and from her, I took in the accompanying, which currently shows up on paper interestingly.

About the centre of the most recent century, when my relative was in her teenagers, a few companions of hers, the O'Connor's, were living in a huge moulded ranch style home, somewhere close to Ballintoy and Hospital in the County of Limerick. The family comprised of Mr. O'Connor., who had been something in India in his childhood and was currently a significant loner, however much regarded locally because of his limited devotion and great heartedness; Mrs. O'Connor., who, notwithstanding her silver hair and wrinkled face, actually held hints of more than normal great looks; Wilfred, an attractive yet determinedly persistent young fellow of between 25 and thirty; and Ellen, a blue-peered toward, the brilliant haired young lady of the genuine Milesian kind of Irish excellence.

My relative was on terms of the best closeness with the entire family, however particularly with the two more youthful society, and it was by and large expected that she and Wilfred would make what is indecently named a "match of it." Indeed, the first of the spooky happenings that she encountered regarding the O'Connor's. happened the very day Wilfred made the since a long time ago expected stride and proposed to her.

It appears to be that my relative was out for a walk one evening with Ellen and Wilfred, when the last mentioned, exploiting his sister's abrupt extravagant for going on to search for canine roses, enthusiastically proclaimed his affection, and, clearly, didn't announce it to no end. The triplet, at that point, in pretty much-lifted spirits—for my relative had given Ellen access to the mystery—headed back home together, and as they were going through a major wooden passage into the nursery at the back of the O'Connor's. home, they saw a tall, spare lady, with her back towards them, burrowing endlessly irately.

"Hello," Wilfred shouted, "who's that?"

"I don't have the foggiest idea," Ellen answered. "It's absolutely not Julia" (Julia was the old cook who, in the same way as other of the workers of that period, didn't limit her work to the culinary workmanship, yet played out a wide range of unspecialized temp jobs too), "nor anybody from the ranch. However, what in heaven's name does she believe she's doing? Hello, there!" and Ellen, raising her normally sweet and melodic voice, gave a little yell.

The lady in a split second turned round, and the triplet got a most savage stun. The light was blurring, for it was late in the early evening, however, what little there was appeared to be focused on the look before them, causing it to seem brilliant. It was an expansive face with exceptionally articulated cheekbones; an enormous mouth, the meagre lips of which were fixed in a shocking and taunting sneer; and extremely pale, sideways set eyes that gleamed perniciously as they met the look of the three presently dismayed observers.

For certain seconds the abhorrent glancing animal remained in dead quiet, clearly boasting over the vexation her appearance had delivered, and, at that point, abruptly bearing her spade, she headed gradually in the opposite direction, turning around once in a while to project a similar noxious happy gander at them, until she went to the fence that isolated the nursery from a long-neglected stone quarry, when she appeared abruptly to disappear in the now dubious sundown, and vanish.

For certain minutes nobody talked or blended, however kept looking after her in a sort of incapacitated bewilderment. Wilfred was quick to end the quietness.

"What a horrendous looking witch," he shouted. "Where's she gone?"

Ellen whistled. "Ask another," she said. "There's no place she might have gone besides into the quarry, and my lone expectation is that she is lying at the lower part of it with a wrecked neck, for I surely never wish to see her again. Be that as it may, come, we should be proceeding onward, I'm cold."

They got going, yet had just continued a couple of yards, when, clearly from the bearing of the quarry, came a chime of giggling, so ridiculing and harmful and by and large malicious, that each of the three automatically stimulated their means, and, simultaneously, ceased from talking, until they had arrived at the house, which they hurriedly entered, safely shutting the entryway behind them. They at that point went directly to Mr. O'Connor. furthermore, asked him who the elderly person was whom they had quite recently seen.

"What was she like?" he questioned. "I haven't approved anybody yet Julia to go into the nursery."

"It unquestionably wasn't Julia," Ellen reacted rapidly. "It was some frightful old hag who was burrowing away like anything. On our methodology, she left off and gave us the most underhanded look I have at any point seen. At that point, she disappeared and appeared to evaporate in the support of the quarry. We thereafter heard her give the most horrifying and seriously fiendish snicker that you can envision. Whoever right?"

"I can't figure," Mr. O'Connor. answered, looking fairly curiously pale. "It is nobody whom I know. Perhaps she was a drifter or wanderer. We should take care to keep every one of the entryways bolted. Whatever you do, don't refer to a word about her to your mom or Julia—they are both apprehensive and effectively scared."

Every one of the three guaranteed, and the matter was then permitted to drop, however my family member, who got back before it got very dim, consequently discovered that evening, sometime after the O'Connor, the family had all resigned to rest, many rings of a similar diabolical ridiculing giggling were heard, simply under the windows, as a matter of first importance in the front of the house, and afterwards in the back; and that, on the morrow, came the news that the business worry in which the greater part of Mr. O'Connor's. cash was contributed had gone crush and the family were essentially poverty-stricken.

The house currently was in unavoidable peril of being sold, and numerous individuals imagined that it was just to turn away this fiasco and to empower her folks to keep a rooftop over their heads that Ellen acknowledged the considerations of an extremely obscene parvenu (an Englishman) in Limerick, and at last wedded him. Where there is no affection, nonetheless, there will never be any satisfaction, and where there isn't in any event, "preferring," there is regularly disdain; and for Ellen's situation disdain, there was no doubt. Scarcely capable, even from the first, to endure her better half (his number one stunt was to have intercourse to her in broad daylight and practically at the same time menace her—likewise out in the open), she at the end developed to severely dislike him, and finally, unfit to persevere through his despised presence any more, she absconded with an official who was positioned around there. The prior night Ellen made this stride, my family member and Wilfred (the last was accompanying his life partner home after a lovely evening spent in her organization) again heard the malicious chuckling, which (although they could see nobody) sought after them for some distance along the twilight paths and across the regular prompting where my relative resided. After this, the chuckling was not heard again for a very long time, yet toward the finish of that period, my general had another experience of the wonders.

She was again going through the evening with the O'Connor, and, on this event, she was talking about with Mr. and Mrs. O'Connor. the approach of Wilfred, who was relied upon to show up home from the West Indies any time inside the following not many days. My relative was not unnaturally intrigued, as it had been orchestrated that she and Wilfred ought to wed, at the earliest opportunity after his appearance in Ireland. They were each of the three—Mr. and Mrs. O'Connor. furthermore, my family member—occupied with vivified discussion (the elderly individuals had surprisingly obtained a significant amount of wealth, and that, as well, had extensively added to them gladness), when Mrs. O'Connor., liking she heard somebody calling to her from the nursery, got up and went to the window. "Harry," she shouted, actually watching out and unfit to eliminate her look, "do come. There's the most terrible elderly person in the nursery, gazing hard at me. Speedy, both of you. She's completely horrendous; she alarms me."

My family member and Mr O'Connor. without a moment's delay jumped up and rushed to her side, and, there, they saw, looking up at them, the paleness of its cheeks increased by a wanderer moonbeam which appeared to be focused exclusively on it, a face which my relative perceived quickly as that of the lady she had seen, two years prior, diving in the nursery. The old witch appeared to recall my family member, as well, for, as their looks met, a sparkle of acknowledgement crawled into her light eyes, and, after a second, offered a path to a statement of such underhanded disdain that my general automatically seized Mr O'Connor. for assurance. Noticing this activity, the animal scoffed awfully, and afterwards, drawing a sort of wrap or hood firmly over its head, moved away with a sort of skimming movement, evaporating cycle a point of the divider.

Mr. O'Connor. without a moment's delay went out into the nursery, at the same time, following a couple of moments, returned, pronouncing that, even though he had looked toward each path, not a hint of their evil-looking guest could he see anyplace. He had scarcely, nonetheless, completed the process of talking, when, obviously from near the house, came a few rings of the most unpleasant giggling, that ended in one uproarious, delayed howl, unquestionably dismal and threatening.

"Gracious, Harry," Mrs. O'Connor. shouted, nearly blacking out, "what can be its importance? That was no living lady."

"No," Mr. O'Connor. answered gradually, "it was the Banshee. As you probably are aware, the O'Connor. Banshee, for reasons unknown or another, has an ingrained contempt of my family, and we should get ready again for some abhorrent news. In any case, he continued, steadying his voice with an exertion, "with God's effortlessness we should confront it, for whatever happens it is His Divine will."

A couple of days after the fact my family member, as might be envisioned, was immensely stunned to hear that Mr. O'Connor. had been sent word that Wilfred was dead. He had, it showed up, been blasted down with fever, expected to have been gotten from one of his travellers, and had kicked the bucket on the very day that he ought to have arrived, on the very day, truth be told (as it was a short time later learned from an examination of dates), whereupon his folks and life partner, together, had heard and seen the Banshee.

Not long after this troubled occasion my general left the area and went to live for certain companions close to Dublin, and however, occasionally, she related with the O'Connor, she never again heard anything of their Banshee.

This equivalent relative of mine, whom I will currently call Miss Sinead (she never wedded), was familiar with two old lady women named O'Rourke who, numerous years prior, lived in a semi-withdrew house near Lower Merrion Street. Miss Sinead didn't know to what in a particular part of the O'Rourke's they had a place, for they were hesitant as to their family ancestry, however, she accepted they initially came from the south-west and were indirectly associated with her very own portion individuals.

As to their home, there positively was an unconventional thing, since in it was one room that was constantly kept bolted, and regarding this room, it was said there existed a secret of the most terrible and frightening depiction.

My general regularly had it barely out of reach of her mind to allude to the room, just to perceive what impact it would have on the two old women, yet she would never entirely summarize the fortitude to do as such. One evening, be that as it may when she was approaching them, the subject was brought to their notification in an exceptionally alarming way.

The senior of the two sisters, Miss Georgina, who was directing at the coffee table, had quite recently given Miss Sinead some tea and was going to spill out another for herself, when into the room, with her cap all astray and her eyes swelling, surged one of the workers.

"Wow!" Miss Georgina shouted, "anything that's the matter, Bridget?"

"Matter!" Bridget answered, in a brogue which I won't endeavour to emulate. "Somebody has entered into that room you generally keep bolted and is making the fiend of a clamour, enough to bring every one of the Saints up in Heaven. Norah" (Norah was the cook) "and I both heard it—a moaning, and a laughing, and scratching, as though the crater was destroying the sheets and breaking all the furnishings, and meanwhile keening and chuckling. For the love of Heaven, women, come and hear it for yourselves. Such goings-on! Ochone! Ochone!"

The two women, Miss Sinead said, turned destructive pale, and Miss Harriet, the more youthful sister, was near the precarious edge of tears.

"Where is the cook?" Miss Georgina, who was by a wide margin the more grounded disapproved of the two, abruptly said, tending to Bridget. "On the off chance that she is higher up, advise her to descend immediately. Miss Harriet and I will take a quick trip and see what the clamour is that you grumble about higher up. There truly is no compelling reason to make this unsettling influence"— here she expected a demeanour the very pinnacle of seriousness—"it's certain to be either mice or rodents."

"Mice or rodents!" Bridget repeated. "I'm upset for the mice and rodents as make every one of those clamours. 'Tis some shrewd soul, sure, and Norah is in total agreement," and with those splitting words she hammered the entryway behind her.

The sisters, at that point, asking to be pardoned for a couple of moments, left the room and returned instantly thereafter looking horrendously white and troubled.

"I'm certain you should think this extremely odd," Miss Georgina saw with as extraordinary a level of unconcern as she could accept, "and I feel we owe you a clarification, however, I should implore you won't rehash an expression of what we advise you to any other person."

Miss Sinead guaranteed she would not, and afterwards, get it together to tune in.

"We have in our family," Miss O'Rourke started, "a most horrendous connection; all in all, a most unsavoury

Banshee. Being Irish, you won't giggle, obviously, as numerous English individuals do, at what I say. You know just as I do, maybe, that a significant number of the truly antiquated Irish families have Banshees."

Miss Sinead gestured. "We have one ourselves," she commented, "however implore go on. I'm seriously intrigued."

"All things considered, in contrast to the greater part of the Banshees," Miss Georgina proceeded, "our own is dreadfully revolting and malicious; so horrible, without a doubt, that to see it, even, is some of the time lethal. One of our extraordinary incredible uncles, for example, to whom it once showed up, is accounted for to have kicked the bucket from stun; a comparative destiny surpassing another of our predecessors, who likewise saw it. Luckily, it appears to have a solid fascination looking like an old gold ring that has been in the ownership of the family for days of yore. The two progenitors I have alluded to are asserted to have been wearing this ring at the time the Banshee appeared to them, and it is said to rigorously bind its signs to the quick area of that article. That is the reason our folks consistently kept the ring stringently secluded, in a bolted room, the key of which was never, briefly, permitted to be out of their ownership. Furthermore, we have arduously followed their model. That is the clarification of the secret you have without a doubt caught wind of, for I accept—because of the workers—it has become the tattle of half Dublin."

"Furthermore, the commotion Bridget alluded to," Miss Sinead dared to comment, fairly hesitantly, "was that the Banshee?"

Miss Georgina gestured. "I dread it was," she noticed seriously, "and that we will instantly know about an overall's demise or grave calamity to some individual from the family; likely, a cousin of our own in County

Galway, who has been sick for certain weeks, is passing on."

She was part of the way right, albeit the last infer was not right. Inside a couple of days of the Banshee's visit an individual from the family kicked the bucket, however, it was not the wiped-out cousin, it was Miss Georgina's sister, Harriet!

THE FOREIGN BANSHEE

As I have commented in a past part, the Banshee today is heard more regularly abroad than in Ireland. It follows the fortunes of the genuine old Milesian Irishman—the genuine O and Mc, none of your tainted Walters or Occasion's—all over, even to the Poles.

Woman Wilde, in her "Antiquated Legends, Mystic Charms and Superstitions of Ireland," cites the instance of a Banshee frequenting that was capable by a part of the Clan O'Grady that had gotten comfortable Canada.

The spot picked by this family for their home was uniquely wild and confined, and one night at two o'clock, when they were all in bed, they were stirred by a boisterous cry, coming, evidently, from right external the house. Nothing coherent was articulated, just a sound demonstrative of the best sharpness and distress, for example, one may envision a lady would offer vent to, however just when in the misery of brain, nearly outside human ability to comprehend.

The impact created by it was one of great dread, and all appeared to feel instinctual that the source from which it radiated was separated from this world and had a place entirely and exclusively to the Unknown. By and by, from what Lady Wilde says, we are directed to gather that a comprehensive pursuit of the premises was made, coming about, as was normal, in complete inability to track down any actual office that could in any capacity represent the cry.

The next day the top of the family and his oldest child went drifting on a lake close to the house, and, although it was their goal to do as such, didn't get back to supper. Different individuals from the family were shipped off the search for them, however not a single hint of them was to be seen anyplace, and no answer for the secret concerning what had befallen them was approaching, till two o'clock that evening, when, precisely 24 hours after the cry had been heard, a portion of the searchers returned, holding on for them the wet, dishevelled, and inert groups of both dad and child. At that point, by and by, the bizarre and unfavourable sound that had so alarmed them on the earlier night was heard, and the distress-stricken family—in other words, the individuals who were left of it—concurring since the Banshee had without a doubt visited them, recalled that their dearest father, whom they had quite recently lost, had frequently talked about the Banshee, as having frequented their part of the group for endless ages.

Another instance of Banshee eerie, that I have as a primula concern, identifies with a part of the southern O'Neill's that got comfortable Italy a decent numerous year prior. It was advised me in Paris by a Mrs. Dempsey, who guaranteed me she had been an onlooker of the marvels, and I currently record it on paper interestingly.

Mrs. Dempsey, while remaining once at an inn in the north of Italy, seen among the visitors an older man, whose extremely stamped highlights and seriously pitiful articulation immediately stood out for her. She saw that he kept altogether reserved from his visitors, and that, each evening after supper, he resigned from the drawing-room, when espresso had been given round, and headed outside and remained on the veranda sitting above the shore of the Adriatic.

She made requests concerning his name and history and was informed that he was Count Fernando Aioli, a well-off Florentine resident, who, having however as of late lost his significant other, to whom he was given, normally didn't wish to participate in the overall discussion. After hearing this Mrs. Dempsey was like never before intrigued. It was not so extremely since a long time ago she, as well, had lost her accomplice—a spouse to whom she was quite joined—and, therefore, it was in a thoughtful state of mind that, seeing the Count go out, not surprisingly, one evening, on to the veranda, she set out to follow him, to attempt, if conceivable, to get into a discussion with him.

With this end in see, she was going to pass the boundary of the veranda, when, to her amazement, she saw the Count was not there alone. Remaining close by, with one hand laid caressingly on his shoulder, was a tall, thin young lady, with masses of the most flawless red-gold hair hanging free and coming to her abdomen. She was wearing an emerald green dress of some dingy substance; yet her arms and feet were uncovered, and stuck out so plainly in the delicate brilliance of the moonbeams, that Mrs. Dempsey, who was a craftsman and had concentrated on the Continent, seen with a rush that they equalled, assuming, to be sure, they didn't outperform in excellence, and she had at any point run over either in Greek or Florentine model.

Much confounded concerning who a strangely attired guest on such amicable footing with the Count could be, Mrs. Dempsey stayed briefly watching, and afterwards, apprehensive in case she ought to stand out for them as begotten, apparently, in the demonstration of spying, she pulled out.

The second she got back again into the drawing-room, notwithstanding, she made to some degree resentful requests of a woman who by and large sat close to her at dinners, for the character of the young lady she had quite recently seen remaining alongside the, said to be, heart-broken Count in a disposition of such close closeness.

"A lady with the Count!" was the answer. "Definitely Not! Who would she be able to be, and how was she?"

Mrs. Dempsey depicted the outsider in detail, yet her companion, shaking her head, could just recommend that she was some newcomer, some visitor who had shown up at the lodging, and gone on the veranda while they were at supper. Feeling somewhat inquisitive, in any case, Mrs. Dempsey's companion strolled towards the veranda, and, in an extremely brief timeframe, returned, looking fairly astounded. "You more likely than not been mixed up," she murmured, "there is nobody with Count Aioli now, and, on the off chance that anybody had left away, we ought to have seen them."

"I'm very certain I saw a lady there," Mrs. Dempsey answered, "and one little while back; she probably got out by one way or another, although there is, evidently, no alternate path than through this room."

As of now, the Count, going into the room, sat down next to them; and the subject must be dropped.

The following evening, notwithstanding, the occasions of the former night were rehashed. Mrs. Dempsey followed the Count on to the veranda, saw the young lady in green remaining with her hand on his shoulder, returned and disclosed to her neighbour at dinners, and the last mentioned, on hurrying to the veranda to look, again returned pronouncing that the Count was separated from everyone else. After this, a slight fight occurred between the two women, the one announcing her conviction that it was every one of an optical hallucination concerning the next, and the other vehemently keeping up with her account that she had seen the young lady she had depicted.

They separated that evening, both somewhat unsettled, however neither would let it out and the next night,

Mrs. Dempsey, when she saw the Count go on to the veranda, gotten her companion.

"Presently," she said, "accompany me and see with your own eyes."

The two women, appropriately, went to the veranda and, opening the entryway tenderly, peeped in.

"There she is," Mrs. Dempsey murmured, "remaining similarly situated."

The sound of her voice, however so low as to be barely heard even by the woman remaining close to her, apparently pulled in the consideration of both the young lady and the Count, for they turned around all the while.

At that point, Mrs. Dempsey, whose look was exclusively focused on the young lady, saw a face of practically unbelievable magnificence—having conveniently etched, yet in no way, shape or form icily old-style highlights, long eyes of a great blue, a smooth wide temple, and carefully and quietly shaped mouth; it was the essence of a young lady, scarcely out of her youngsters, and it was loaded up with a demeanour of endless distress and love.

Mrs. Dempsey was delighted to the point that, to cite her own words, she "stood looking at it in astounding wonder and surprise," and may, maybe, have been looking at it actually, had not the voice of the Count got back to her to earth.

"I trust, women," he was saying, "that you don't see anything bizarrely upsetting in my appearance tonight, for me without a doubt appear to be the object of your concern. May I inquire as to why?"

Even though he talked graciously, even the bluntest might have seen that he was quite irritated. Mrs. Dempsey along these lines rushed to answer.

"It isn't you," she stammered out, "it is the woman—the woman you have with you. I—I liked I knew her."

"The woman I have with me," the Count shouted, in accents of cold amazement. "Benevolently clarify what you mean?"

"Why the woman?" Mrs. Dempsey started, and afterwards she looked round.

The Count was remaining before her—however, he was very alone. There was no remnant of a young lady dressed in green, nor of some other individual on the veranda saving themselves, and promptly underneath it, a good way off of in any event thirty feet, flickered the white shingles of the quiet and abandoned—totally abandoned—beach.

"She's gone," Mrs. Dempsey cried, "yet I'm good I saw her—a woman in green remaining close to you." Then, interestingly, she felt apprehensive and shuddered.

The Count, who had been noticing her intently, presently progressed a stage or two towards her, and in an altogether different tone said:

"If you don't mind, kindly depict the woman? Is it safe to say that she was old or youthful, dull or reasonable?"

"Youthful and reasonable, extremely reasonable," Mrs. Dempsey shouted. "However, if it's not too much trouble, come inside, for I've gotten something of a stun, and can, maybe, converse with you better in the gaslight, with individuals close by whom I know are people."

He did as she mentioned, and turned out to be increasingly more intrigued as she continued with her depiction, intruding on her every so often with questions. Was she certain the young lady had blue eyes, he asked, and how is it possible that she would determine what shading the eyes were by the light of the moon just; Mrs. Dempsey's answer to which being that the young lady's entire body appeared to be enlightened from the inside, in such a way that everything about being seen, nearly, if not exactly, as plainly as though she had been remaining in the full glare of electric light? At the finish of her account, Mrs. Dempsey was additionally addressed by the Count.

"Had she," he asked, "at any point been informed that he was part of the way Irish, since," he added, on getting a negative answer, "I'm, and my genuine name is O'Neill, my extraordinary incredible granddad having expected the name of Aioli to come into some property when the family, which came from the south of Ireland, gotten comfortable Italy, many, numerous years prior. Yet, what will, I am certain, be of extensive interest to you is the way that this part of the O'Neill's, the branch to which I have a place, is spooky by a Banshee, and that that Banshee has, I accept—since its depiction given me by different individuals from my family counts with the portrayal you have given me of the young lady you saw remaining by me—appeared to you. I would add that it never uncovers itself, except for when an O'Neill is going to pass on, and as I am a remarkable last of my line, I can't consider any justification it having in this way seemed three evenings in progression, except if it is to foresee my end."

Mrs. Dempsey was not for a long time ago left in question. On the morrow, the Count was called to Venice on critical business, and on his way to the rail line depot he unexpectedly dropped down dead, the fervour and effort having, so it was assumed, demonstrated a lot for his heart, which was known to be powerless.

Supposed to be slipped from the more youthful of the two children of King Milesians, it unquestionably isn't unexpected that the O'Neill's ought to have a Banshee—without a doubt, it would be amazing on the off chance that they didn't—yet I have discovered it to some degree hard to follow. Nonetheless, as indicated by Lady Wilde in her "Irish Wonders,", there is a room at Shane Castle which is stringently saved for it.

The Banshee, Lady Wilde says, is regularly found in this loft, once in a while showing up covered in a dull, fog-like mantle; and at different occasions as a stunning young lady with long, red-gold hair, clad in a red shroud and green kirtle, decorated with gold. Woman Wilde proceeds to reveal to us no damage at any point happens to the Banshee's visit, except if she is found in the demonstration of crying when her cries might be taken as a specific sign that some individual from the family will presently bite the dust. Mr. Michael authenticates this by expressing that on one event one of the O'Neill's of Shane Castle heard the Banshee crying, similarly as he was going to set out on an excursion, and died soon a while later, which is to some degree strange because in most of the cases I have gone over the Banshee doesn't show itself at all to the individual whose passing it predicts. An old, likely the most established, part of the O'Neill's currently dwells in Portugal, however up to the current I have not prevailing with regards to getting any proof to warrant the suspicion that the Banshee frequenting has been known about that country.

To be sure, the Banshee is by all accounts similarly as flighty and unruly as any girl of Eve, for there is no consistency whatever in her developments. The very families one figures she would frequent, she regularly contemplatively stays away from, and not rarely she focuses her consideration on the individuals who are completely dark, but, consistently of true-blue Irish extraction.

INSTANCES OF MIXED UP PERSONALITY

In past parts, I have managed cases that are, without question, those of certified Banshee frequenting. I currently propose to portray a couple of cases which I will term instances of farfetched Banshee frequenting—in other words, instances of frequenting which, although said to be Banshee, can't, taking into account the marvels and conditions, be along these lines assigned with any level of sureness.

In the first place, I will review the case identifying with the Riordan's, a family living in Canada. Their home, a long, low, two-celebrated structure, remained on a desolate spot out and about prompting Montreal, and a young woman, whom I will assign Miss Delaney, was visiting them when the episodes I am going to describe occurred.

The climate had been more than ordinarily fine for that season, yet finally, the inescapable and undeniable indications of a break had set in, and one evening dark veils of mist accumulated in the sky, the breeze whistled inauspiciously in the fireplaces and viciously shook the kaleidoscopic maple leaves, while, after a period, the moon, which had been balancing like an incredible red globe over St Lawrence, turned out to be unexpectedly clouded, and enormous drops of downpour came spluttering against the windows.

Miss Delaney, who had been seized with abnormal fretfulness which she was unable to shake off, at that point went into the lobby and was going to address one of Major Riordan's nieces, who were likewise on a visit there, when her consideration was captured by the sound of a substantial carriage blundering along with the more respectable option, from the heading of Montreal, at an incredible rate. It being presently almost ten o'clock, an hour when there was generally next to no traffic, she was fairly amazed, her surprise expanding significantly when she heard the wheels crunching on the rock drive, and the carriage quickly moving toward the house.

"Clearly, it is past the point of no return" she started, however, was stopped by the Major, who, unexpectedly pushing past her to the front entryway, similarly as the carriage drew up, swung it to, and, in shuddering flurry, bolted, and banned, and darted it.

Strides were then heard hastily rising the means to the front entryway, and promptly subsequently a progression of uproarious rodent tat-tats, even though, as everybody in a flash recollected, there was no knocker on the entryway, the Major having had it taken out numerous years prior, for an explanation he either couldn't or would not clarify.

Frightened practically insane by the clamour, the entire family had in no time flat amassed in the lobby, and they currently stooped, clustered together, while the Major in a voice which, regardless of the way that it was raised to its most noteworthy pitch, could scarcely be heard over the irate and excited thumping, the Almighty to ensure them.

As he kept asking the rodent tats steadily became feebler and feebler, until they at long last stopped, after which the strides were indeed heard on the stone advances, this time plunging, and the carriage drove away. It was not, in any case, until the resonations of the wheels could presently don't be heard that the Major rose from his knees. At that point, offering his family do moreover, he demanded that they ought to immediately resign, without talking a word, to their rooms; and prohibited them at any point to specify the make a difference to him once more.

When Miss Delaney and the Major's nieces were in their room—they divided a room among them—they hurried to the window and watched out. The sky was very clear now, and the moon was sparkling forward in all the quality of its quiet cool magnificence; however, the grounds and street past were very abandoned; not a remnant of any individual or carriage could be seen anyplace, and, on the morrow, when they rushed the first floor and inspected the rock, there were no signs whatever of any wheels.

The day passed predictably, and by and by it was evening; the Major had perused supplications as normal at around ten, and the family, additionally obviously, had resigned to rest. Miss Delaney, who was utilized to a lot later hours, thought that it was hard to get it together to rest unexpectedly early, however, she had quite recently figured out how to nap off, when she was excited by her companion Ellen, the senior of the Major's two nieces, pulling savagely at her bedclothes, and, on looking into, she saw a tall figure, clad in what resembled cloister adherent's articles of clothing, strolling across the room with long, subtle steps. As she looked at it in winded shock, it abruptly stopped and, turning its hooded head round, gazed steadily at Ellen, and afterwards, proceeding onward appeared to dissolve into the divider. At all occasions, it had evaporated, and there was nothing where it had been standing, saving twilight.

For certain minutes Ellen was too panicked to even consider talking, yet she finally shouted to Miss Delaney and beseeched her to come and get into her bed, as she not, at this point challenged lie there without help from anyone else.

"Did you see how it took a gander at me," she murmured, gripping hold of Miss Delaney, and shivering fiercely. "I don't figure I will at any point get over it. We should leave here tomorrow. We should, we should," and she burst out crying.

As might be envisioned, there was little rest for both of the young ladies again that evening, and it appeared to them as though the morning could never come; yet, when finally, it came, they revealed to Major Riordan what had occurred, and pronounced they truly tried not to go through one more night in the house.

Even though bothered on hearing what they needed to say, the Major didn't squeeze them to change their choice and stay, yet disclosed to them that to go, he thought, considering the present situation, was far the most astute and most secure thing for them to do. An hour or so later, having completed their pressing, they were every one of the three going for the last walk together in the nursery, when they liked they heard somebody pursuing them down one of the walkways, and, turning round, they saw the figure that had upset them in the evening, standing not far behind them.

The daylight falling straightforwardly on it uncovered highlights now just excessively effectively recognizable of somebody since a long time ago dead, yet vivified by a soul that was completely adversarial and pernicious, and as they shrank back alarmed, it extended forward one of its long, hard arms and contacted first Ellen and afterwards her sister on the shoulder. It at that point veered round, and, moving away with similar curiously long and clandestine steps, appeared out of nowhere to amalgamate with the shadows from the trees and vanish.

For certain minutes the young ladies were incapacitated with dread to do other than remain where they were, shuddering; however, their resources finally reasserting themselves, they made an unexpected scramble for the house and ran at maximum velocity till they arrived at it.

It was half a month a short time later, nonetheless, and not till at that point, that Miss Delaney, who was back again in her home in Ireland, gotten any clarification of the wonders she had seen. It was given her by a companion of the Riordan's who turned out to visit one of Miss Delana's family members in Dublin.

"What you saw," this companion of the Riordan's said to Miss Delaney, "was, I accept, the Banshee, which consistently shows itself before the passing of any individual from the family. Once in a while, it screeches, similar to the yelling of a lady who is as a rule brutally done to death, and in some cases, it simply gazes at or contacts its casualty on the shoulder with its skeleton hand. Regardless its approach is deadly. Just," she added, "let me entreat you never to hint even the slightest bit at this to the Riordan's, as they never notice their phantom to anybody."

Miss Delaney guaranteed, simultaneously communicating a sincere expectation that the marvels she had seen didn't highlight the sickness or passing of both of her companions; however in this, she was destined to the most profound disillusionment, for inside half a month of the date whereupon the Banshee—if Banshee it truly were—had shown up, she got greetings of the passing's of both Ellen and her sister (the previous capitulating to an assault of some harmful fever, and the last to a mishap), and what's more, heard that Major Riordan had kicked the bucket too. As Major Riordan could never examine the subject of his family apparition with anybody by any stretch of the imagination, it is difficult to say whether he accepted the frequenting to be a Banshee eerie or not; yet some trusted it to be this sort of frequenting, and I should say I think they weren't right.

In the first place, the Riordan's was Anglo-Irish. Their association with Ireland may have gone back a century or somewhere in the vicinity, however they were unquestionably not of Milesian nor even Celtic Irish plunge; and, thus alone, couldn't have obtained a Banshee frequenting. Also, the Banshee that we know doesn't show up, as the Riordan's apparition showed up, attired in the garments of a strict request; and the mentor or funeral wagon ghost (which in the Riordan's case went before the indication of the alleged Banshee) is in no way, shape or form an extraordinary frequenting; and since it is as a rule joined by wonders of the sepulchral sort (the sort saw by Miss Delaney and the Major's nieces), it could be said to establish in itself a curious type of family frequenting which isn't, obviously, solely kept to the Irish.

Thus, I completely excuse the hypothesis that the famous Riordan's phantom had anything at all to do with the Banshee. À propose of mentors, I am helped to remember an occurrence related by that past expert of the unusual, J. Sheridan Le Faun, in a short story named

"A Chapter in the History of a Tyrone Family." As it identifies with that kind of apparition that is so regularly stupidly mistook for the Banshee, I figure I can't show improvement over give a concise sketch of it.

Miss Richardson, a youthful Anglo-Irish young lady, dwelled with her folks at Ash town, Tyrone, and her senior sister, who had as of late wedded a Mr. Carew of Dublin, being normal with her significant other on a visit, extraordinary arrangements were walking for their gathering.

They were leaving Dublin by mentor on Monday morning, they had written to say, and wanted to show up at Ash town sometime the next day. The morning and evening passed, in any case, with no indication of the Carew's, and when it got dim, and still they didn't come, the Richardson family started to feel a triviality uncomfortable.

The night was fine, the sky cloudless, and the moon, when it finally rose, couldn't have been more splendid. It was a still evening, as well, so still that not a leaf mixed, who were stressing their ears to the most extreme, probably got the sound of a moving toward vehicle on the more responsible option, had there been one, when it was still a way off of a few miles. Be that as it may, no stable came, and when suppertime showed up, Mr. Richardson, just like he won't, made a visit through the house, and painstakingly secured the shades and bolted the entryways. Still, the family tuned in, and still, they could hear nothing, nothing, either close to or distant.

It was presently midnight, however, nobody hit the hay, for all were lightened with the urgent expectation that something must finally occur—either, the actual Carew's would abruptly turn up, or a courier with a letter clarifying the deferral.

Neither outcome, notwithstanding, happened, and nothing happened until Miss Richardson, who had, for the occasion, permitted her psyche to harp on an extraordinary theme, gave a beginning. Her heartbeat uproarious, and she held her breath! She heard carriage wheels. Indeed, undoubtedly, she heard wheels—the wheels of a mentor or carriage, and they were getting increasingly particular. In any case, she stayed quiet. She had been censored more than once for giving a bogus caution—she would now let another person talk first. Meanwhile, endlessly came the wheels, halting briefly while the iron door at the passage to the drive was swung open on its corroded pivots; at that point endlessly once more, stronger, stronger and stronger, till all could recognize, amid the yelping of the canines, the sound of dispersed rock and the snapping and washing of the whip. There was not even a shadow of a doubt now, and with upbeat cries of "It is them! They have come finally," an ordinary charge was made for the lobby entryway, guardians and sister, workers and canines, competing with each other to see who could arrive first. However, lo and view, when the entryway was opened, and they ventured out, there was no indication of a mentor or carriage anyplace; nothing was to be seen except for the wide rock drive and grass past, land with moonbeams and inhabited with eccentric shadows, yet quiet, with a quietness that proposed a churchyard.

The entire family currently took a gander at each other with white and bewildered faces; they started to be apprehensive; while the canines, running about, and sniffing, and crying, were anxious and apprehensive, as well.

Finally, a sort of frenzy set in, and all made a scramble for the house, taking consideration, when once inside, to close the entryway with much more noteworthy scurry than they had shown in opening it. The family at that point resigned to rest, yet not to rest, and promptly the following morning they got the news that completely validated their premonitions. Mrs. Carew had become sick with fever on Monday, while arrangements for the takeoff were being made, and had died, likely at the exact second when the Richardson's, hearing the ghost mentor and confusing it with a genuine one, had opened their lobby entryway to invite her.

That is the essence of the episode as related by Mr. Le Faun, and I have cited it simply to show how an instance of this sort, particularly when it occurs in Ireland, and to a family that has for quite a while been related with Ireland, may now and again be confused with a certified Banshee frequenting, even though, obviously, there is no explanation whatever to assume that Mr. Le Faun himself toiled under any hallucination as to it, or proposed to pass on to his peruses an impression of the frightful that the conditions didn't warrant. He simply states it as an instance of the extraordinary without endeavouring to relegate it to an exceptional class.

Woman Wilde in her "Antiquated Cures, Charms and Usages of Ireland," p, 164, cites another instance of mentor frequenting in Ireland, an entirely horrible one; while in a book named "Meanders aimlessly in Northumberland," by a similar writer, we are educated, "when the demise funeral wagon, drawn by headless ponies and driven by a headless driver, is seen about midnight continuing quickly, yet without commotion, towards the churchyard, the passing of some impressive personage in the ward makes certain to occur at no far off period." Also, there is a ghost of this portrayal that is infrequently seen out and about close to Langley in Durham, and my family members, the Vises of Limerick—in any event, so my grandma, née Sally Vise, used to say—are spooky by an apparition mentor as well; for sure, there is by all accounts no limit to this sort of frequenting, which is in every case either exceptionally beautiful or extremely startling, and in some cases both pleasant and unnerving.

Simultaneously, albeit seriously intriguing, presumably, the ghost mentor isn't Irish, and not at all associated with the Banshee. To act as an illustration of the limit tension of certain individuals to be believed to be of old Irish extraction and to have a Banshee, I may allude to an occurrence regarding Mrs. Elizabeth Sheridan, which is recorded in references on pages 32 and 33 of "The Memoirs of the Life and Writings of Mrs. Frances Sheridan," aggregated by her granddaughter, Miss Alicia Leano, and distributed in 1824, and quote from it the accompanying:

"In the same way as other Irish women who dwelled during the early piece of life in the nation, Miss Elizabeth Sheridan was a firm devotee to the Banish, a female demon, joined to old Irish families. She genuinely kept up that the Banish of the Sheridan family was heard howling underneath the windows of Qualco before the news showed up of Mrs. Frances Sheridan's passing at Blois, consequently bearing the cost of them a supernatural suggestion of the approaching despairing occasion. A niece of Miss Sheridan's driven her extremely mad by seeing that as Miss Frances Sheridan was by birth a Chamberlain, a group of English extraction, she reserved no privilege to the guardianship of an Irish pixie, and that, in this manner, the Banish probably committed an error."

It is a fairly inquisitive, and, maybe, a not very verifiable truth, that a few families have two Banshees, an amicable and a threatening one; while a couple, however, a couple of just, have three—an agreeable, an unpleasant, and an impartial one. An instance of the two Banshees bringing about a double Banshee frequenting was advised me as of late by a man whom I met in Paris at Henriette's in Montparnasse. He was a Scot, a writer, of the name of Menzies, and his story concerned an Irish companion of his, additionally a columnist, whom I will call O'Hara.

From what I could assemble, these two men were inverse. O'Hara—kind, imprudent, and liberal to some extent; Menzies—to some degree chilly, cautious concerning cash, and incredibly wary; but, aside from their work which was the clear connection between them, they had one trademark in like manner—the two of them venerated pretty ladies. The high forehead and outrageous women's activist with her apathetic highlights and seriously scornful grin was a bad dream to them; they looked for continually something satisfying, and humble, and liberated from scholastic feelings of pride, and they discovered it in Paris—at Henriette's.

It so happened one day that, incapable to get a table at Henriette's, the spot being packed, they meandered along the Boulevard Montparnasse and transformed into another café near the Boulevard Rasp ail. This spot, as well, was full, yet there was one little table, at which sat alone a young lady, and, at O'Hara's idea, they immediately made for it.

"You shrewd individual," Menzies murmured to his companion after they had been situated a couple of moments, "I know why you were so restless to come here."

"Indeed, wasn't I right," O'Hara, whose eyes had not even once left the young lady's face, reacted. "She's the prettiest I've seen for some days."

"Not awful!" Menzies replied, to some degree fundamentally. "Yet, I don't care for her mouth, it's wolfish."

O'Hara, notwithstanding, could see no deficiency in her; the more he looked at her, the more profound and more profound he fell head over heels in love; not that there was anything exceptionally uncommon in that, since O'Hara was no sooner off with one fire than he was on with another; and he arrived at the midpoint of in any event a few love cases a year. In any case, to Menzies this most recent undertaking was irritating; he realized that when O'Hara lost his heart, he, by and large, lost his head as well, and would never talk or think on any subject yet the eyes, hair, mouth and finger-nails—for, like most Irishmen, O'Hara had energy for very much kept, all around framed hands—of his new heavenly nature, and on this event, he needed O'Hara to staying normal somewhat more.

It was, at that point, thus essentially, that Menzies didn't get a little energized over the new disclosure, as well; for he will undoubtedly concede that, notwithstanding the lupine articulation about the mouth, there was some pardon this time for his companion's energy. The young lady was pretty, a practically wonderful blonde, with gently moulded hands, and dressed as just a youthful Paris magnificence can dress, who has cash and recreation at her order.

Indeed, there was pardon; but then it was the stature of indiscretion. Young ladies mean consumption somehow, and a little while ago neither he nor O'Hara had anything to spend. While he was thinking, nonetheless, O'Hara was acting.

He offered the young lady a cigarette, she smilingly dismissed it; however, the ice was broken, and the discussion started. There is no compelling reason to go into a specific regarding what followed—it was what consistently continued for a situation of this portrayal—dazzle fixation that constantly finished with surprising unexpectedness; just in this occurrence the fascination was blinder than any time in recent memory, and the closure, however abrupt, was not common. O'Hara asked the young lady to supper with him that evening.

She acknowledged, and he took her out again the next evening. From that second all explanation left him, and he surrendered himself to the maddest of distraught interests.

Menzies saw little of him, however whenever they did by chance end up gathering it was consistently the normal, worn-out storey—Gabrielle! Gabrielle Delacour. Her star-like eyes, flawless hair, etc.

At that point came a night when Menzies, burnt out on his own organization, strayed to Montmartre, and met an individual comrade of his, by name Douglas.

"I say, old individual," the last commented, as they lolled over a little marble-bested table and watched the advancements of a more than typically challenging vaudeville artiste, "I say, what about that Irish buddy of yours, 'O' some random thing. I saw him here a few evenings ago with Marie Diblanc."

"Marie Diblanc!" Menzies verbalized. "I have never known about her."

"Not knew about Marie Diblanc!" Douglas shouted. "Why I thought each columnist in Paris knew about her, yet maybe she was before your time, for she's had a lovely long spell of jail—in any event, five or six years, which as you probably are aware is quite firm these days for a lady—and has as of late come out. She was very much a youngster when they sacked her, however a youngster with a psyche as old as Brownville's in wrongdoing and bad habit—she burglarized and everything except killed her mom for a couple of Louis, other than fashioning checks and taking discount from shops and lodgings. They say she was in with the very most noticeably awful hoodlums in Europe and outperformed them all in nuance and challenging. At the point when I saw her a few evenings ago her hair was coloured, and she was wearing the holiest person like articulation; however, I knew her no different either way. She was unable to mask her mouth or her hands, and it is those highlights that I notice in a lady more than everything else."

"Depict her to me," Menzies said.

"A brunette initially," Douglas answered, "however now a blondie—masses of extravagantly waved brilliant hair; exceptionally long eyes—rather excessively seriously blue and far separated for my preferring—a very much shaped mouth, however, the lips are extremely slight, and part with her on the double."

"That is the young lady," Menzies shouted determinedly. "That is the young lady he calls Gabrielle Delacour. I was with him the day he initially met her— over in Montparnasse." Douglas gestured.

"Believe it or not," he said. "That is the name he acquainted her with me by. However, I'm very sure she's Marie Diblanc; and I figure you should give him the tip. On the off chance that he's seen about with her, he'll be suspected by the police. Additionally, she makes certain to perpetrate some wrongdoing—for a young lady with that sort of face and history never changes, she continues being directly down terrible as far as possible—and get him involved. Just, conceivably, she will utilize him as her apparatus."

"I'll see him and caution him," Menzies said. "I'll call at his place tonight, however, there's no knowing when he'll turn up, for he's the most unpredictable animal under the sun."

Consistent with his promise, Menzies, following a couple of more minutes' discussion, got up and backtracked his means to Montparnasse. O'Hara lived in the Rue Campagna Première, near the celebrated "hare warren." His entryway, as not rarely occurred, was opened, yet he was out. Menzies went in, and, going into the little room which filled in as a parlour, lounge area, and study joined, hurled himself entirely into a rocker and lit a cigarette. He didn't try to illuminate as it was a twilight evening, and the obscurity fit his present temperament. Inevitably, notwithstanding, feeling somewhat cold, he turned on the gas fire, and afterwards, looking at the clock over the shelf rack, seen it was close on twelve.

Right then and there was a clamour outside, and, thinking it was O'Hara, he called out, "Hello, Bob, is that you?"

As there was no reaction he called once more, and this time there was a giggle—a terrible, vindictive sort of laugh that took Menzies to leap up immediately and indignantly request who was there. Nobody answering, he went to the room entryway, and, opening it wide, saw a couple of yards from him a tall dull figure encompassed in what gave off an impression of being a shroud and outfit.

"Hello!" he cried. "Who are you, and what the — do you need here?"

Whereupon the figure drew to the side its covering and uncovered a face that made Menzies utter a shout of fear and spring back. It was the substance of an elderly person with high cheekbones, taut wilted skin, and sideways set pale eyes that sparkled perniciously as they met Menzies' stunned gaze. A disarranged mass of tangled yellow hair delegated her head and plummeted most of the way to her shoulders, uncovering, in any case, her ears, which stood apart conspicuously from her head, colossal and pointed, similar to those of a huge wolf. A leaderish white sparkle appeared to exude from inside her and to increase the overall ghastliness of her appearance.

Although Menzies had never put stock in apparitions, he felt certain since he was taking a gander at something which didn't have a place with this world. It was, he certified, so totally shocking that he would have expressed a petition and offered it begone, had not his words passed on in his throat so he was unable to verbalize a sound. He at that point attempted to lift a hand to cross himself, yet this, likewise, he couldn't do; and the lone thing he discovered he could do, was to gaze at it in idiotic, surprised loathsomeness and marvel.

How long this situation may have gone on it is difficult to say; yet at the sound of weighty and human strides, first in the lower part of the structure, and afterwards climbing the stone flight of stairs prompting this level, the elderly person vanished, evidently amalgamating with the fairly creative hangings on the divider behind her. Menzies was all the while scouring his eyes and looking when O'Hara burst in upon him.

"Hello, Donald, is that you?" he started. "I've done it." "Done what?" Menzies stammered his nerves all at any rate.

"Why, proposed to Gabrielle, obviously," O'Hara went on enthusiastically, "and she's acknowledged me. She, the prettiest, best, best little colleen I've at any point run over, has disclosed to me she will wed me. Ye divine beings, I will go off my head with happiness; go obvious, gazing frantic, I advise you." And intersection the floor of the examination he tumbled into the seat Menzies himself had quite recently involved.

"I say, old individual, why not salute me?" he proceeded.

"I do salute you," Menzies noticed, sitting down. "Obviously I compliment you, however, are you certain she is such a young lady you will consistently think often about or who will consistently think often about you. You haven't known her extremely long, and most ladies cost a deuced part of cash, particularly French ones. Try not to make the permanent strides before thinking about them well first."

"I have," O'Hara countered, "so it's no utilization lecturing. I have decided to wed Gabrielle, and not one thing in existence will hinder me."

"Do you know her kin or anything about them?" Menzies wandered. O'Hara giggled.

"No," he said, "yet that doesn't trouble me in the smallest. I shouldn't mind whether her dad was a navy or a publican, or whether her mom took in washing and squeezed a couple of odd shirts and socks from time to time, just as it occurs, they don't influence the inquiry by any stretch of the imagination, since they are both dead. Gabrielle is a vagrant—very all alone—so I have entirely protected the extent that that goes. No bombastic dad to counsel, no grouchy old relative to fear. Gabrielle was instructed at a community school, and, however you may chuckle, knows close to nothing of the world. She's just about as guiltless as a butterfly. We are to be hitched one month from now."

Finding that it was no natural use to say anything else regarding the matter, all at once on all occasions, Menzies changed the discussion and alluded to the occurrence of the elderly person. O'Hara immediately got intrigued.

"Why," he said, "from your depiction, she probably been one of the Banshees that should frequent our family, and which my mom consistently proclaimed she saw quickly before my dad's passing. A revolting witch with a stunning head of tow-hued hair, who remained on the flight of stairs snickering wickedly, and afterwards, at the same time, evaporated. She is known as the awful Banshee to recognize her from the great one, which is, so I have consistently been directed to see, extremely wonderful, yet which never shows itself, saving when anything particularly frightful will happen to an O'Hara."

Feeling uncomfortable in his psyche, Menzies currently bid his companion a great evening and returned home.

After that, days passed and Menzies saw nothing of O'Hara, until one evening, when he was figuring it should be about since the marriage was to occur, O'Hara turned up at his level, and recommended that they should take a walk around the course of the fortresses close to Montour's. However, O'Hara was not in his typical positive feelings; he appeared to be extremely melancholy and discouraged, and Menzies assembled that there had been incidental contrasts of assessment between his companion and Gabrielle and that the issue was not running very as easy as it may. Gabrielle had a considerable number of admirers, one of them rich, and O'Hara was irritated at the considerations they had been giving on his life partner, and at the way where she had gotten them. Be that as it may, there was something different, as well; something he could find in his companion's face and way, however, which O'Hara would not really as alluding to. Menzies was satisfied, for there now appeared to be a good omen that these erosions would emerge into something more grounded and more positive, and lead to a crack that would be conclusive.

He was so engaged in theories of this nature that he disregarded the time or where they were, and was simply taken back to earth by the whistle and yell of a train, which made him immediately acknowledge they had left Montour's and were a few miles without the strongholds.

It was likewise getting very sunset, and, as he must be up curiously promptly toward the beginning of the day, he proposed to O'Hara they would do well to turn around. They were then close next to a bunch of brambles and an elevated pine tree that was adapting back and forth in such an unconventional way that Menzies' consideration was immediately coordinated to it.

"What's up with that tree?" he commented, pointing at it with his stick.

"What's up with the tree?" O'Hara snickered. lit's not the tree, there's anything the matter with the trees okay, very OK. —it's you. What in heaven's name would you say you are gazing at it for in that absurd style? Have you unexpectedly gone distraught?"

Menzies made no answer, however, went up to the tree and analyzed it. As he was doing as such, a slight unsettling influence in the shrubs made him look around, and he saw, a couple of feet from him, the tall figure of a young lady, clad in a sort of long streaming mantle, however with uncovered head and feet. The evening glow was all over, and Menzies, hard and troublesome however he was, generally speaking, to please, acknowledged it was beautiful, undeniably more dazzling, so he pronounced a while later, than any lady's face he had at any point looked at. The eyes especially dazzled him, for, albeit in the haziness he was unable to tell their shading, he could see that they were of a very excellent shape and setting, and appeared to be loaded up with distress that was practically beyond what her heart could bear. In fact, so piercing was this distress of hers, that Menzies, tainted by it, as well, couldn't hold back the tears from his own eyes; and, dismal and apathetic as he was essentially, his entire being out of nowhere turned out to be in a real sense saturated with pity and pity.

The young lady gazed directly toward him, yet just for a couple of moments; she at that point turned towards O'Hara and appeared to focus her entire consideration upon him. There was currently, Menzies thought, a specific vagary and a something shadowy about her that he had not from the outset seen, and he was figuring how he could test her to check whether she was actually a substance or just an optical dream, when O'Hara, who was getting worn out at his long nonattendance, called out, whereupon the young lady without a moment's delay disappeared, articulating, as she dissolved away behind the scenes, in a similar peculiar way as the elderly person had done, a horrendous, nerve-racking, howling scream, that it appeared to fill the entire air and to wait on forever.

Completely alarmed, Menzies, when his dispersed faculties could gather themselves, escaped from the spot, and didn't stop running till O'Hara's furious yell carried him to a halt. To his wonder, O'Hara hadn't heard anything and was just irritated at his distraught conduct. In solution to his depiction of the young lady, nonetheless, and the howling, O'Hara without a moment's delay pronounced it was the Banshee, and the one he had consistently been so especially restless to see.

"Except if you are having a joke to my detriment," he said, "and you look excessively terrified for that, you have really seen her—a wonderful young lady, dressed after some bygone era Irish custom, in a free streaming green mantle—just obviously you were unable to see the tone—with head and feet exposed. Yet, it's odd about that howl. The great Banshee in a family is constantly expected to make it, however for what reason didn't I hear her? For what reason would it be a good idea for it to just be you? You're Scotch, not Irish."

"For which I'm genuinely grateful," Menzies said with warmth. "I've lived while never seeing or hearing an apparition or anything moving toward one for a very long time, and now I've seen and heard two, inside the short space of three weeks, and all as a result of you, since you're Irish. Not this time. None of your Banshees for me. I'd prefer, multiple times rather, be only a conventional lady from the Highlands, and get rid of your exceptionally refined and critical family apparition."

"Come, presently," O'Hara said great humoredly, "we will not squabble about so unsubstantial a thing as the Banshee. How about we pick up the pace and have a jug of cognac to make us consider something rather livelier."

Menzies regularly thought about those words, for it isn't the most frivolous words and activities that frequent our memory furthest degree in after days. The remainder of the evening passed tediously, and, after they had "toasted" one another, the two companions isolated for the evening.

After two days O'Hara's body lay in the Morgue, whither it had been taken from the Seine. Even though there were a few questions communicated regarding the specific way wherein he had met his demise, it was formally recorded "passing from misfortune," and it was not till quite a long while later Menzies took in reality.

He was then in Mexico, in a little town not twenty miles from San Blas, on the Western Coast, accomplishing some paperwork for a South American paper. A vendor and his better half were killed; done to death in a uniquely coldblooded way, in any event, for those parts, and one of the professional killers was found in the act.

The other, a lady, prevailing with regards to getting away. As there had been such countless homicides recently around there, the residents proclaimed they would make an exceptionally serious illustration of the guilty party, and hang him, immediately, on the location of his malicious shock. Menzies, who had never seen anything of the sort, and was, obviously, on edge for duplicate, took great consideration to be available. He stood very near the bound man and got each expression of the admission he made to the nearby padre. He gave his name as André Decamps, his age as 25, and his ethnicity as French. He attested that he was initial actuated to take to wrongdoing through becoming hopelessly enamoured with a famous French criminal of the name of Marie Diblanc, who acknowledged him as her darling, restrictively on his joining the band of Apaches of which she was the perceived pioneer.

He did as such and forthwith dove into each sort of insidiousness possible. Among different wrongdoings in which he was ensnared, he referenced that of the homicide of an Irishman of the name of O'Hara, who should have met with an incidental demise from suffocating in the Seine. What truly occurred, so the youthful bandit said, was this. M. O'Hara was frantically enamoured with Marie Diblanc, who was acting to him like

Gabrielle Delacour, an honest young lady from the country, when she was a lot of engaged and was being looked for high and low, at that very time, by absolutely more than one frantic spouse. All things considered, one day she convinced M. O'Hara to take her to a dance given by some exceptionally affluent companions of his.

He did as such, and she imagined, obscure to him, to carry me in, and between us, we wandered off with something like 10,000 pounds of gems.

M. O'Hara came to presume her—how I don't have a clue, except if he caught some wanderer discussion among her and some other individual from our pack at one of the cafés they used to feast at. In any case, she became more acquainted with it, and on the double made plans to have him put far removed. It was orchestrated that she ought to get him to a house Montmartre, where a few of us were secluded from everything, and that we should both slaughter and cover him there.

All things considered, he came, and, on seeing that he had fallen into a snare, bethought her, if his life should be relinquished—and, in any case, presently he realized she was a cheat he wouldn't have it in any case—to take it herself. This she, at last, consented to do, and, lying in her arms, he permitted her to press a toxin sack over his mouth, thus put him to death. His body was taken to the Seine that evening in a fiacre and dropped in. Decamps added that it was the lone event whereupon he had seen Marie Diblanc truly moved, and he accepted she was a triviality attached to the Irishman, in other words, on the off chance that she could be partial to anybody.

Menzies, who was profoundly intrigued, separated each molecule of data he could out of the man, yet nothing would cause the last to concede a word with regards to what had happened to Diblanc." If I get lost," he said, "she is sure to go there, as well; for terrible as I am, I trust her to be boundlessly more regrettable; more awful, multiple times more awful than any Apache man I have at any point met. But then, corrupted and abhorrent as she is, I love her, and will never realize a subsequent satisfaction till she goes along with me."

The man passed on; and Menzies, as he sketched his swinging body, felt altogether fulfilled finally that the apparition he had seen outside the fortresses of Mansouri's was the acceptable and delightful Banshee, the Banshee that possibly showed itself when some surprisingly horrendous destiny was going to overwhelm an O'Hara.

HAPPENING IN SPAIN

Another instance of double Banshee frequenting that happens to me, occurred in Spain, where so many of the most seasoned Irish families have settled and was identified with me by an inaccessible association of mine—an O'Connell. He all around recalled that he said, numerous years prior, when he was a kid, his dad, who was an official in the Carlist Army, advising him of an experience that happened to him during the principal flare-up of the Civil War. His dad and another youngster, Dick Flanagan, were subalterns in a ranger's regiment that took a conspicuous part in a frantic commitment with the Queen's Army. The Carlists were being driven back, when, as a final frantic asset, their uncovered small bunch of mounted force charged and promptly turned the fortunes of the day. In the warmth of the affray, nonetheless, Ralph O'Connell and Dick Flanagan, diverted by their excitement, got isolated from the remainder of the corps, and were, therefore, overwhelmed by sheer numbers and taken detainees.

In those days much ruthlessness appeared on one or the other side, and our two legends, beaten, and wounded, and starving, were hauled along in a half-swooning condition, amid the insults and gibing's of their captors, till they were, at last, stopped in the messy prison of an old mountain palace, where they were educated, they would be kept till the hour designated for their execution. The second they were distant from everyone else, they put forth the most arduous attempts to loosen the straps of extreme cowhide with which their hands and feet were so cold-bloodedly bound together, and, after numerous wild-eyed undertakings, they finally succeeded. Flanagan was quick to get free, and when his desensitized appendages permitted him to do as such, he crept to the side of his companion and freed him, as well. They at that point inspected the room decently well in obscurity and chose their lone any expectation of break lay in the stack, which, fortunately for them, was one of those antiquated designs, adequately wide to concede the entry of a mature individual. Ralph started the climb first, and, after a few vain endeavours, during which he knocks and wounded himself and made such a clamour that Flanagan dreaded he would be heard by the gatekeeper outside, he ultimately figured out how to get traction and gain adequate headway for Flanagan to continue afterwards.

In all that they did that evening karma supported them. On arising out of the stack on to the top of the palace, they were cheered to discover a tree becoming so close to one of the dividers that they had little trouble in grasping hold of one of its branches thus diving in wellbeing to the ground. The watchmen were sleeping, in any event, none were to be seen anyplace, thus, feeling their path circumspectly in and out a thick development of trees and shrubberies, they before long avoided the premises, and got themselves indeed free, however in a piece of the country with which they were absolutely unacquainted. Two hours slogging along a convoluted, uneven more respectable option, or to give it a more suitable name, track, for it was not all that much, finally carried them to a wayside hotel where, regardless of the high-level hour—for it was somewhere in the range of one and two AM—they resolved to hazard request for a night's haven. I say "hazard" because there was a solid soul of partisanship abroad, and it was very pretty much as likely as not that the hotel individuals were followers of the Queen.

Ralph thumped over and over, and the entryway was finally opened by a little youngster who, holding a candle in one hand, sluggishly scoured her eyes with the other and, in rather irritable tones, asked what the men of their word implied by going to the house at a ridiculously early time and awakening everybody. Ralph and Flanagan were so struck by her appearance that for certain seconds they could just stand expanding at her, denied of all forces of discourse. Such a dream of beauty neither of them had seen for some a difficult day, and both were more than usually vulnerable where the reasonable sex was concerned. Dull, as the greater part of the young ladies are in Spain, she was not dark, but rather had, then again, a most uniquely reasonable composition, without that propensity to furriness which is obvious in so many of the ladies of that country. Her highlights were, maybe, a triviality too intense, yet in severe extent, and her eyes a small piece hard, however, the shape and shade of them—by candlelight a practically purplish dim—were independently wonderful. She had bright white teeth, as well, however, there was a something about her mouth, in the setting of the lips when they were shut for example, and in the overall articulation, that baffled Ralph, and which was bound to get back to his psyche ordinarily a while later.

Ralph saw that her hands were not those of a labourer class, of a class that needs to do a lot of harsh and difficult work, yet that they were white furthermore, very much kept, the fingers tightening and the nails long and almond moulded. She wore a few rings and wristbands, and appeared to be by and large not quite the same as the sort of young lady one would have expected to discover in an exceptionally honest sort of building, arranged, as well, in a distant spot.

Ralph was not exactly as indiscreet as his companion, and although, as I have said, truly defenceless, was not so far drove away by his sentiments as to be through and through unequipped for perception.

His initial feelings of the young lady were that, even though she was uncommonly lovely, there was something—separated even from her mouth—that he was unable to comprehend, and which caused him dubious anxiety; he saw it especially when her look meandered to their movement stained regalia, and immediately landed on Flanagan's single ring, which contained a ruby and was a sort of family mascot, much the same as the well-known catch of Count Daniel

O'Connell of Tricone; and she mumbled something which Ralph liked had reference to "Carlists," and afterwards, as though cognizant he was watching her, she raised her eyes rapidly and, in tons of tired apathy, this time asked what the noblemen needed. Ralph quickly answered that they required a bed with breakfast, not very early, and, maybe, later on—lunch meeting. He added that if the motel was full, they wouldn't at all see any problems with resting in a horse shelter or stable.

"All we need," he said, "is to rests somewhere with a rooftop over our heads, for we are frightfully drained."

At the notice of a stable the young lady grinned, saying she could offer them something preferably better over that; and, offering both follow her higher up, with as little clamour as could be expected, she led them to a huge room with an extremely low roof, and, having saved the candle on a dresser, she wished them great evening and quietly pulled out.

"Maybe better than our late quarters in the jail," Ralph shouted, taking an overview of the loft, "however a small piece desolate."

"Gibberish!" Flanagan countered. "The lone miserable things here are your considerations. I need to remain here consistently, for I never saw a prettier young lady or a cosier-looking bed."

He started to strip down as he talked, and shortly both young fellows were loosened up at full length sleeping soundly.

Around two hours after the fact Ralph got up with a brutal begin to hear particular hints of strides pussyfooting their route delicately along the section outside towards their room entryway. In a moment every one of his resources was on the caution, and he sat up in bed and tuned in. At that point something blended in the corner by the window, and, looking around there, he saw to his shock the figure of a tall thin young lady, in a long, free, streaming outfit of some dim material, with a pale face, wonderfully etched, however in no way, shape or form stringently old-style highlights, and masses of sparkling brilliant hair that fell in undulating disarray on to her neck and shoulders. The possibility that she was the Banshee immediately happened to him. From his dad's depiction of her, for his dad had frequently addressed him about her, she and the excellent lady, whom he was presently taking a gander at, were surely a lot of the same; moreover, like the Banshee, when his dad saw her, was crying, and this lady was crying—crying most sharply, her entire body influencing back and forth as though racked with the most strong distress—he couldn't resist the urge to imagine that the personality between them was set up and that they were, truth be told, indeed the very same individual.

As he was all the while looking at her with the most significant pity and appreciation, his consideration was abruptly coordinated, by an odd scratching sound, to the window, where he saw, squeezed against the glass, and gazing directly in at him, a face which is everything about the most alarming differentiation to that whereupon his eyes had, yet a second prior, been devouring. It was underhanded to the point that he felt sure it could just exude from the least Inferno, and it sneered at him with such horrifying danger that, bold man as he had substantiated himself on the field of fight, he currently totally lost his nerve, and would have called out, had not the two figures unexpectedly evaporated, their vanishing being quickly trailed by the most anguishing, sad shouts, blended with uproarious giggling and fiendish laughing, which, for the occasion, totally deadened him. The shouts proceeded for certain seconds, during which time each molecule of blood in Ralph's veins appeared to freeze, and afterwards, there was quietness—profound and sepulchral quietness. Reluctant to be any more in obscurity, Ralph leapt up and lit the flame, and, as he did as such, he unmistakably heard strides move briskly away from the entryway and go covertly pussyfooting down the section.

As might be envisioned, he didn't rest again for quite a while, not, without a doubt, until sunshine, when he step by step fell into a rest, from which he was in the long run stimulated by noisy bangs on the entryway, and the voice of the lovely motel lady declaring that the time had come to get up.

After breakfast he portrayed his involvement with the night to Flanagan, who, fairly to his wonder, didn't snicker, yet shouted truly:

"Why, you have seen our Banshee. At any rate, the young lady dressed in green is our Banshee. I saw her before the passing of a cousin of mine, and she appeared to my mom the night before my dad kicked the bucket. I don't have the foggiest idea what the other nebulous vision might have been, except if it was what my dad used to term the 'contemptuous Banshee,' which he said was simply expected to show up before some exceptionally unpleasant fiasco, more awful even than death if anything could be more regrettable."

"You haven't the imposing business model of Banshees," Ralph giggled. "We have one as well, and I am positive the lady I saw—the excellent lady I mean— was the O'Connell Banshee. I would have you realize that the Limerick O'Connell's, with whom I am associated, are very as old a family as the Flanagan's; they are, in reality, straightforwardly dropped from Niall of the Nine Hostages."

"So are we," Flanagan addressed fervently, at that point, he burst out chuckling. "All things considered, well," he said, "extravagant quarrelling about anything as unimportant as a Banshee. In any case, on the off chance that they were Banshees that you saw the previous evening, they're somewhat out in their estimations. They ought to have preceded that clash, not after it; except if it's the passing of some relative of one of us they're forecasting. I trust it's not my sister."

"I don't envision it has anything to do with you," Ralph answered. "They were both taking a gander at me."

He was going to say something further, when Flanagan, seeing the little youngster come into the space to gather up the morning meal things, on the double started conversing with her; and as it was very much apparent that he needed the field to himself, for he was head over ears in adoration, Ralph got up and reported his goal of going for a stroll around the premises.

"Try not to go in the wood, Senior, whatever you do," the young lady noticed, "for it is swarmed with rascals. They don't meddle with us since we were once acceptable to one of their wiped-out society—and the Spaniard, rascal however he might be, always remembers a consideration—yet they assault outsiders, and you will be very much encouraged to keep to the more respectable option."

"Which is the closest town?" Ralph requested.

"Trujillo," the young lady replied, a similar inquisitive articulation crawling at her that had perplexed Ralph such a great amount previously, and which he discovered difficult to dissect. "It is around eight miles from here. Wear Hurtado, the Governor, is a Carlist, and was engaging some Carlist officers there yesterday."

"Great!" Ralph shouted. "I will stroll there. Will you accompany me, Dick, or will you stand by here till I return. I don't assume I will be back much before the evening."

"Gracious, don't rush," Flanagan chuckled, looking at the young lady blissfully, "I'm completely cheerful here, and need a rest seriously. Don't, whatever you do, let on to anybody associated with central command where we are. Release them on envisioning, for some time, we are dead."

"The Seniors have been in a fight, yes?" the young lady intruded, timidly.

"A fight," Flanagan chuckled, "not half one. We were taken detainees and just avoided hanging through my unmatched brains and persistence. In any case, I don't at all weep over the dangers and difficulties we have gone through, for, had occasions turned out else, we ought to never have had the delight of seeing you, Sanora," and seizing her hand before she could forestall him, he squeezed it intensely to his lips, covering it with kisses.

Thinking it was high an ideal opportunity to be off, Ralph presently took his flight. A few hours' strolling carried him to Trujillo, where, yet for a fortunate episode, he may have wound up arrived stuck. As he was entering the edges of the town, he met an old labourer, faltering under a sack of onions, and no sooner did the last see his uniform than he immediately called out:

"Senior, on the off chance that you esteem your freedom, you will not enter Trujillo around there. The Governor is the nemesis of all Carlists, and has provided severe orders that, anybody with leanings towards that gathering will be put collared immediately."

"Are you certain?" Ralph shouted. "I was advised it was only the alternate route about, and that he was a solid disciple of our motivation."

"Whoever revealed to you that, lied," the elderly person reacted, "for he had a nephew of mine shot just the previous morning for saying in open he trusted that pathetic quitter of a lady would before long be put off the seat and we ought to have somebody fit to administer—which means Don Carlos—in her place. Accept my recommendation, Senior, and either change those garments without a moment's delay or give Trujillo as wide a compartment as could be expected."

Ralph at that point inquired as to whether there was any spot close by where he could buy a regular citizen suit, and, on being educated that there was a Jew's shop inside a couple of moments' walks, he said thanks to the elderly person most genially for giving him so well disposed an admonition, and on the double continued there.

To spare the gritty details he purchased the garments and, in this way masked, went on into the town, and, with the object of getting any data he could concerning the adversary's powers, he ate at the key inn, and listened mindfully to the discussion that was occurring surrounding him. Later on, in the day some Christion troopers showed up, officials on the staff of one of the Royalist commanders, and Ralph chose to stay in the lodging for the evening and check whether he could get hold of some truly clear news that may be of worth to his base camp. Discovering that somebody would leave the lodging quickly and passing by the hotel where Flanagan was remaining, he gave them a note to provide for his companion, expressing that he was unable to be back till the next day, maybe about early afternoon. He at that point took up his seat before the parlour shoot, evidently retained in perusing the most recent notice from Madrid, yet keeping his ears well open for any discussion that may merit interpreting in his wallet. Nor was he baffled, for the Christion warriors waxed loquacious over a portion of mine host's best port, and revealed numerous insider facts concerning the developments of the Queen's powers, that would have involved a court military, had it yet gone to the notification of their general.

That evening, however, the room he was given was very splendid and lively and different from the one he had involved the night before, his psyche was so brimming with dismal dread that he discovered it very difficult to rest. He continued thinking about the vision he had seen—that flawless, pixie face of the young lady with the brilliant hair, her charming eyes, her magnificent, though extremely human mouth; she was so awesome, so celestial, so loaded with scrumptious compassion and pity; so dissimilar to any natural lady he had at any point met; and afterwards that other face—those seriously malicious, light green eyes, that vile taunting mouth, that confusing mass of tangled, tow-hued hair.

It was excessively horrible—excessively incomprehensibly foul and pernicious to dare consider, and seized with an attack of shivering, he pushes his head under the bedclothes, in case he should see it again showing up before him. What, he pondered, did they forecast? Not some frightful happening to Dick. He had consistently perceived that the person who neither sees nor hears the Banshee during its indications is the one that is bound to kick the bucket. But Dick was definitely as protected in that motel as he was here— here, encompassed on all sides by his adversaries. More than once he liked he heard his name called, thus reasonable was it, that, careless of his fear of seeing something sinister in the room, he finally sat up in bed and tuned in. Everything was still, be that as it may; there were no sounds by any means; none whatever, saving the delicate murmuring of the breeze, as it cleared delicately past the window and the distant hooting of a night bird. At that point, he set down once more, and again there appeared to come to him from someplace extremely close within reach a voice that verbalized unmistakably and mournfully his name—Ralph, Ralph, Ralph! — multiple times one after another, and afterwards stopped. Nor did he hear it once more.

Worn out and unrested, he rose early and, covering his bill, set off with long, quick walks toward the wayside motel. There was a quality of superb harmony and serenity about the spot when he showed up. Every one of the sunbeams appeared to have congregated in that one spot and to have changed over the dividers and window-sheets of the little older style incorporating into sheets of shined gold. Birds twittered joyfully on the tree-tops and under the overhang of the rooftop, and the most delectable smell of honeysuckle and roses penetrated the entire environment.

Ralph was charmed, and all his inauspicious premonitions of the prior night were in a split second scattered. The house was named "The Travelers' Rest"; it may even have been styled "The Travelers' Paradise," for all appeared to be so quiet and tranquil—so genuinely sublime. He rapped at the entryway, and, after certain minutes, rapped once more. He at that point heard strides, which some way or another appeared to be oddly natural, warily tag along the stone section and respite at the opposite side of the entryway, as though their proprietor were in question if to open it.

Again, he rapped, and this time the entryway was opened, and the young lady showed up. She looked rather pale, however, was a lot of sprucer and more intelligent than she had been when Ralph last saw her. She wore a charming sort of tramp gown of red velvet—the skirt short and the bodice decorated with masses of sparkling silver coins, while her feet were clad in extremely savvy, petite shoes, additionally red, with large silver clasps.

"Your companion's gone," she said. "He appeared to be extremely irritated with your not turning up the previous evening, and disappeared straightforwardly after breakfast."

"In any case, didn't he get my note?" Ralph shouted, "and didn't he leave any message?"

"No, Senior," the young lady answered. "No note came for him, yet he said he would attempt to bring in, here again, tomorrow morning, to check whether you had shown up."

"What's more, he didn't say where he had gone?" "No."

Ralph looked at her curiously. She positively was brilliantly lovely, and, radiant to relate, didn't smell of garlic. Indeed, he would remain, and attempt to go under the interest of her excellence as Dick had done. But then, why had Dick gone off in such a rush? How had this naive animal dealt with annoying him? Ralph realized Flanagan was on occasion able to be finished imprudent and hurried in his affection makings. Had he got on all in all too quickly? Spanish young ladies are effortlessly disturbed, and maybe this one had a darling behind the scenes. Maybe she was hitched. That appeared to him the most possible clarification for Dick's nonappearance. To be irritated at his not turning up the previous evening was all rubbish. Ralph knew his companion dreadfully well for that. In any case, he chose to remain, and the young lady offered him the room he and Dick had recently involved. Just, she clarified, he should not go in it till later on in the day, as it would have been cleaned.

After lunch get-together, which he plunked down to alone, as the young lady, notwithstanding his squeezing greeting, would not participate in the supper with him, on the request that she had numerous things to take care of, he went a little far up the slope at the rear of the premises and appreciated a peaceful break under the shadow of the trees. He rested for such a long time that the nightfall had very much set in before he arose and by and by made tracks for the hotel.

This time he entered by an entryway in the back of the house, and, in a little cleared patio, saw the young lady, habited in somewhat more workaday clothing, yet with her hair still teasingly adorned with strips, honing a long sparkling blade on a major pounding stone, which she was turning all around with the expertise of a past fancy woman of the craftsmanship.

"Hello!" he shouted. "What are you up to? Not honing that cutting edge to leave me with, I trust."

"The Senior has known about pigs," the young lady answered, getting defensive in a grin, nearly adding up to a smile. "Indeed, I will murder one tonight."

"Great sky!" Ralph discharged, looking warily at the white, adjusted arms and the long, thin, tightening fingers. "You execute a pig! Do you do practically everything in this house? Is there nobody else here to help you?"

"Goodness, indeed, Senior," the young lady chuckled. "There is Isabella, an elderly person who comes here consistently to do all the hard harsh work, and my auntie, yet there are sure positions they can't do because their visual perception isn't generally excellent, and their hands come up short on the expertise. The courteous fellow looks stunned, however, is there anything so frightful in executing a pig? One cut and it is rapidly done—rapidly. We need to live by one way or another, and, all things considered, the Senior is an officer—he follows the livelihood of slaughtering!"

"Goodness, indeed, it is all very well for enormous, harsh men. One by one way or other partners them with deeds of savagery and carnage. In any case, with excellent, modest young ladies like you, it is unique. You should shiver at the considered blood, and be all pity and empathy."

"However, not for pigs," the young lady snickered, "nor for Seniors. Presently kindly go in and sit in the parlour, or my auntie will hear me conversing with you and blame me for burning through my time."

Ralph hesitantly complied, and drawing his seat close up to the parlour fire—for the mid-year nights in Spain are frequently crisp—was soon profoundly ingested in plans and theories regarding what's to come. After dinner, when the little youngster came into the space to tidy up the table, Ralph saw that she was indeed wearing the gay clothing she had worn before in the day; and all in red, even to the strips in her hair, she was by all accounts dressed more teasingly than any other time in recent memory. She was likewise disposed to be more open, and in light of Ralph's challenge to participate in a glass of wine with him, she brought a rocker and came and planted it close alongside him.

Pretty as he had suspected her previously, she presently appeared to him to be indefinably stunning, and the more he gazed at her, gazed into the profundities of her enormous, delightfully formed purplish dim eyes, the increasingly more pitifully oppressed did he become, till, eventually, he understood she had him totally at her kindness, and that he was almost frantically and urgently enamoured with her.

They drank together, thus ingested was he in looking at her eyes—surely, he never stopped looking at them—that he didn't see what he was drinking or how often she topped off his glass. If she had given him a harmed cup, it would have been no different either way, he would have depleted it off and kissed her mind and feet with his perishing breath.

"Presently, Senior," she said finally after he had held her hand to his lips and in a real sense covered it in kisses, "presently, Senior, it is the ideal opportunity for you to head to sleep. We don't keep late hours here, and tomorrow, Senior, on the off chance that he is as yet in the same perspective, will possess a lot of energy for rehashing to me his estimations."

"Tomorrow," Ralph stammered. "Tomorrow, that is a huge way off, and isn't it tomorrow that that individual Flanagan is coming?"

The young lady snickered. "Indeed," she said boldly, "there will be you two tomorrow, the one as terrible as the other, and I thought, Senior, you were the steadier of the two. All things considered, indeed, you are the two officers, and fighters were ever gay canines; yet you should be cautious, Senior, you and your companion don't squabble, for, as you probably are aware, more than one fellowship has been ended through the witching look of a woman's eyes, and you both appear to like investigating mine."

"What!" Ralph faltered furiously. "Did that individual Dick take a gander at you? Did he try to take a gander at you? Damn— — " however before he could express another syllable, the young lady put her delicate little hand over his mouth and pushed him tenderly to the entryway.

Then again making wild love to her and energetically condemning Dick, Ralph at that point permitted himself to be got higher up to his room by pushes and coaxing, and, as he put forth a last unhinged attempt to kiss and caress her, the entryway closed forcefully and he got himself—alone.

For certain minutes he stood pulling and contorting at the entryway handle, and afterwards, finding that his endeavours had no impact, he was faltering off to the bed intending to get into it similarly as he was, the point at which he got his foot on something and fell with a collide with the floor, striking his face intelligently on the edge of a seat. Briefly or so he was incompletely paralyzed, yet, the progression of blood from his nose easing him, he continuously woke up, all hint of his intoxication having disappeared. The main thing he did then was to take a gander at the rug which, by a fortunate turn of events, was red, a generally articulated, harmful dark red, precisely the shade of his blood. Where he had fallen was near the bed, and, as his eyes meandered along with the rug by the side of the bed, he liked he saw another soggy fix. He immediately got the flame and had a more critical look.

Indeed, there was an incredible sprinkle of dampness on the floor, close to the top of the bed, pretty much in a line with the pad. He applied his finger to the fix and afterwards held it to the light—it was wet with blood.

Loaded up with a nauseating feeling of anxiety, Ralph currently continued to make a cautious assessment of the room, and, lifting the cover of a tremendous oak chest that remained in one corner, he was sickened to see the exposed body of a man lying at the lower part of it, all clustered up.

Tenderly raising the body and bowing down to look at it, Ralph got a subsequent stun. The face that gazed toward him with such utter absence of demeanour in its huge, protruding, shiny eyes was that of the once gay and amusing Dick Flanagan.

The way of his passing was very much self-evident. His throat had been cut, not neatly as a man would have done it, yet with rehashed hacks and slices, that sharp obviously to a lady's handicraft.

This at that point clarified everything, clarified the inquisitive something in the young lady's eyes and mouth he had seen when he previously saw her; clarified, as well, the subtle, pussyfooting strides in the section that evening, the justification the presence of the Banshees, the energy with which the young lady had utilized him with wine, her red dress—and— honorary pathway.

However, why had she done it—for simple shameful burglary, or because they were Carlists. At that point remembering the look she had fixed on the ruby in

Dick's ring, the appropriate response appeared to be clear. It was, obviously, theft. Snake-like, she utilized those excellent eyes of hers to interest her casualties—to quiet them into a misguided sensation that all is well and good; and afterwards, when they had entirely capitulated to adore and wine, of which she gave them their fill, she butchered them.

Murders in Spanish motels were in no way, shape or form exceptional about that time, and even at a lot later date, and had this homicide been submitted by some old and monstrous and abrasive "have," Ralph would not have been astonished, yet for this young lady to have done it—this young lady so youthful and charming, why it was practically incomprehensible, and he would not have trusted it, had not the dreary verifications of it lain so close within reach. What was he to do? Since he was calm and in full ownership of his resources, it was strange for him to fear a young lady, even though she was equipped; yet assuming she had confederates, and it was barely likely she would be separated from everyone else in the house.

No, he should attempt to get away; yet how! He inspected the window, it was vigorously banished; he attempted the entryway, it was bolted outwardly; he looked into the stack, it was very restricted to concede the section of anybody even a large portion of his size.

He was done, and the solitary thing he could do was to pause. To stand by till the young lady pussyfooted into the space to execute, and afterwards—he was unable to bear battling with her, even though she had so merciless killed helpless Dick—make his getaway.

With this end in see, he smothered the candle, and, lying on the bed, claimed to be sleeping soundly.

In about an hour he heard advances, delicate, careful strides, rise the flight of stairs and come taking clandestinely towards his entryway. At that point, they stopped, and he instinctually realized she was tuning in. He inhaled intensely, similarly as a man would do who had flushed not admirably but rather excessively well, and had therefore fallen into a profound rest. By and by, there was a slight development of the entryway handle.

He proceeded with breathing, and the development was rehashed. Even more, blaring breaths, and the handle this time was turned. Delicately he crawled off the bed to the entryway, and, as it gradually opened and a figure in red, looking spooky and vile, sneaked in, so he unexpectedly shot past and scrambled toward the section. There was a wild scream, something zoomed past his head and fell with a boisterous clack on the floor, and every one of the entryways in the house ground floor appeared to open all the while. Arriving at the top of the steps in a couple of limits, he was down them in an instant. A frightful old witch hurried at him with an axe, while another matured animal, whose sex he was unable to decide, pointed a wild blow at him with some other instrument, yet Ralph kept away from them both, and, arriving at the front entryway, which fortunately for him was just bolted, not shot, he was expediently out of the house and into the expansive parkway.

The shouts of the ladies delivering noting echoes from the wood in the hoarser yells of men, Ralph ran away, nor did he quit running until he was well headed to Trujillo. He didn't, in any case, go to the last town, expecting that the hotel individuals may follow him there and get him captured as a Carlist; all things considered, he struck off the more responsible option along a sideway, and, fortunately for him, about early afternoon fell in with a high-level watchman of the Carlist Army.

His inconveniences at that point, for a period, in any event, stopped; however, to his enduring misgiving he was always unable to retaliate for Dick's demise; for when the conflict was finally finished and he had prevailed with regards to convincing the neighbourhood specialists to take the matter close by, the motel was discovered to be unfilled and abandoned. Nor was the lovely murderess at any point seen or knew about again around there.

BANSHEE IN THE WAR

Albeit the Banshee frequenting alluded to in my last section happened during a conflict, the signs didn't occur on the front line; nor were they in reality because of the battling. Simultaneously it can't be rejected that they were its result, for had our two lieutenants not been battling frantically in a conflict and got isolated from the principal body of the Army, more likely than not they could never have visited the wayside motel, and the Banshee indications there couldn't have ever happened.

There are, in any case, numerous cases on record of Banshee appearances happening in the war zone, either preceding or after, or even while the battling was occurring. Mr. Michael, in his "Irish Wonders,", says:

"Before the Battle of the Boyne, Banshees were heard singing noticeable all-around absurd camp, the reality of the prediction being checked by the demise move of the following morning."

Presently my very own few quick progenitors participated in the Battle of the Boyne, and as indicated by a family custom one of them both saw and heard the Banshee. He was sitting in the camp, the night preceding the battling, bantering with a few different officials, including his sibling Daniel, when, feeling a frosty breeze fighting against eminent loss and blowing down his back, he went round to search for his shroud which he had disposed of a brief timeframe previously, attributable to the warmth from a fire close next to them. The shroud was not there, and, as he turned round even further to search for it, he saw to his bewilderment the figure of a lady, wrapped from head to foot in a mantle of some dull streaming material, standing a couple of feet behind him. Pondering who in the world she could be, yet assuming she should be a family member or companion of one of the officials, for her mantle looked expensive, and her hair—of a superb brilliant tint—however hanging free on her shoulders, was all around focused on, he kept on looking at her with interest. At that point he steadily saw that she was shaking—shaking all finished, with what he from the outset envisioned should be chuckling; yet from the consistent grasping of her hands and hurling of her chest, he, at last, understood that she was sobbing, and he was additionally guaranteed on this point, when an abrupt whirlwind, blowing back her mantle, he got a full perspective all over.

Its excellence energized him. Her cheeks were just about as white as marble, however, her highlights were awesome, and her eyes the most beautiful he had at any point seen. He was going to address her, to ask on the off chance that he could be of any support of her, when, somebody calling out and asking him what in heaven's name he was doing, she without a moment's delay started to liquefy away, and, amalgamating with the delicate foundation of dark fog that was crawling towards them from the stream, at long last vanished.

He thought about her, be that as it may, a few hours after the fact, when they were all resting, attempting to grab a couple of hours' rests, and by and by liked he saw, in faint, shadowy layout, her reasonable face and figure, her huge, miserable eyes, looking sadly first at one and afterwards at another of his associates, however especially at one, a simple kid, who was lying enveloped by his military shroud, close next to the seething ashes of the fire. He liked that she moved toward these young people and, twisting around him, stroked his short, wavy hair with her sensitive fingers.

Believing that potentially he may be sleeping and dreaming, he scoured his eyes vivaciously, however, the diagrams were still there, immediately getting more grounded and more grounded, increasingly unmistakable, until he understood with an incredible rush that she was there, similarly as positively as she had been the point at which he had first seen her.

He was so purpose watching her and wishing she would leave the adolescent and come to him, that he didn't see that one of his friends had seen her, as well, until the last mentioned, who had raised himself into a half-sitting stance, talked; at that point, similarly as in the past, the figure of the young lady softened away and appeared to get consumed in obscurity and shadowy foundation.

After a second, he heard, simply over his head, an uproarious groaning and crying that went on for a few seconds and afterwards diminished in one since a long time ago, an extended wail that recommended mental pain of an incredibly miserable and sad nature.

The passing's of the greater part of his allies of the evening, including that of the wavy-haired kid, happened on the next day.

However, the Banshee, even though seeming to troopers of Irish birth just, doesn't bind its considerations to the individuals who are battling on their local soil; it has been expressed that she regularly showed herself to Irishmen connected with on dynamic assistance abroad during the Napoleonic Wars, and to those serving in America during the Civil War.

Concerning the Banshee shows regarding the Napoleonic missions, I have not had the option to get any put-down account; yet as the consequence of various letters conveyed by me broadcast in the journey of data, I was asked by a few groups to call either at their homes or clubs and, readily tolerating their solicitations, I gained from them the episodes which, with their consent, I am currently going to relate.

Miss O'Higgins, a matured woman, dwelling, before the late conflict, near Fifth Avenue, New York, and visiting, when I met her, a companion in the Rue Campagna Première, Paris, disclosed to me that she all around recollected her granddad revealing to her when she was a kid that he heard the Banshee at Talavera, a little while preceding the extraordinary fight. He was presented with the Spanish Army, having hitched the little girl of a Spanish official, and had no clue at the time that there were any men of Irish extraction in his corps. Bivouacking with around 100 different officers in a valley, and ending up getting up in the night with an uncooperative thirst, he advanced down to the banks of the waterway that streamed close by, drank his fill, and was in the demonstration of returning, when he was frightened to hear a most anguishing shout, immediately followed by another, and afterwards another, all procedure obviously from the camp, whither he was wending his means. Considering what in the world might have occurred, and slanting to the conviction that it should be here and there associated with one of those ladies' criminals who slinked about wherever around evening time, looting and killing, with equivalent exemption, any place they saw an opportunity, he stimulated his speed, just to discover, on his landing in the camp, no sign whatever of the presence of any lady, albeit the shouting was going on as enthusiastically as could be expected. The sounds appeared to start things out from one piece of the camp, and afterwards from another, however, to be in every case overhead, as though expressed by imperceptible creatures, drifting at the tallness of approximately six or seven feet, or, maybe, more, over the ground, and although Lieutenant O'Higgins had from the start credited these sounds to one individual just, on listening mindfully he liked he could distinguish a few distinct voices—all women's—and he ultimately arrived at the resolution that at any rate three or four ghosts probably been available. As he remained there tuning in, not knowing what else to do, the howling and wailing appeared to develop increasingly frightening, until it influenced him such a lot of that, solidified as he had become to a wide range of wretchedness and savagery, he, as well, wanted to sob, out of sheer compassion. In any case, this situation didn't keep going long, for at the sound of a rifle fired (that of a guard, as Lieutenant O'Higgins a while later discovered, giving a bogus alert in some inaccessible piece of the camp) the howling and crying unexpectedly and stopped, and was never, the Lieutenant pronounced, heard by him again.

On referencing the make a difference to one of his sibling officials in the first part of the day, the last mentioned, no little intrigued and astounded, immediately said: "You have without a doubt heard the Banshee. Helpless D— —, who fell at Corunna, frequently used to enlighten me concerning it, and, you may rely on it, there are some Irishmen in camp now, and it was their burial service requiem that you tuned in to."

What he said end up being very right, for, on inquisitive, Lieutenant O'Higgins found three of the officers who had been resting around him that evening had Irish names, and were, certainly, of antiquated Irish beginning; and every one of them died on the bleeding field of Talavera, after 24 hours.

A story identifying with an O'Farrell, who was with the Spanish in a similar conflict, was likewise advised me by Miss O'Higgins; yet whether this O'Farrell was the renowned general of that name or not I don't have a clue. The story ran as follows:

It was the day before the fall of Badajoz, and O'Farrell, who was in Badajoz at that point, a detainee of the French, was welcome to participate in dinner with some Spanish-Irish companions of his of the name of McMahon. The French, it very well might be noticed, were, when in doubt, maybe more tolerant to their Irish detainees over to their English, and O'Farrell was permitted to meander aimlessly about Badajoz in wonderful opportunity, a simple promise being removed from him that he wouldn't walk around the limits of the town without extraordinary authorization. On the night being referred to O'Farrell left his quarters cheerful. He preferred the McMahons, particularly the most youthful little girl Katherine, with whom he was especially infatuated. He considered his case sad, in any case, as Mr. McMahon, who was poor, had frequently said none of his little girls ought to wed, except if it were somebody who was sufficiently rich to guarantee them being very much accommodated, should they be left a widow; and as O'Farrell had only his compensation, which was small enough in all heart, he saw no possibility of his always having the option to propose to the object of his expressions of warmth. Had he been solid disapproved of enough, he advised himself, he would have immediately bid farewell to Katherine, and never have permitted himself to see or even think about her again; however, helpless wimp that he was, he was unable to bear bringing a last peep at her—the eyes that he had admired into his paradise and all that made daily routine worth experiencing for— thus he held tolerating solicitations to their home and hurling himself across her way, at whatever point the smallest chance introduced itself.

What's more, presently he got himself again speeding to meet her, disclosing to himself more than once that it ought to be the last time, and yet deciding that it ought to be no such thing. He showed up at the house very right on time, obviously—he generally did—and was appeared into space to stand by them till the family had completed their evening latrines. Huge glass entryways opened out of the room on to a veranda, and O'Farrell, venturing out on to the last mentioned, hung over the iron railings, and looked into the semi-patio, semi- garden beneath, in the focal point of which was a wellspring overcome by the marble sculpture of an exceptionally excellent lady, that his nature advised him was an accurate picture of his darling Katherine. He was looking at it, delighting in the superb expectation of meeting the fragile living creature and blood partner of it in a brief timeframe, when hints of music, of somebody playing an incredibly, tragic and mournful air on the harp, came to him through the open entryway. Much amazed, for none of the family to the extent he knew, were harpists, nor had he, without a doubt, at any point seen a harp in the house, he turned round; at the same time, to add to his wonder, nobody was there. The room was similarly as unfilled as when he had been guided into it, but the music exuded from it. Significantly confused, for occasionally there was a particular far-offences in the sounds which he could compare to nothing he had at any point heard previously, he stayed on the veranda, forestalled by an abnormal sensation of wonderment, and something much the same as fear, from wandering into the room.

He was in this manner involved, half standing and half inclining toward the system of the glass entryway when the harping unexpectedly stopped, and he heard meanings and sobbing starting at a lady experiencing eruptions of the most extreme and fierce misery. Combatting with an extraordinary dread that presently started to hold onto him, he summarized the goal to peep again into the room, however his eyes took in the entire scope of the room, he could see where anybody might be sequestered from everything, and nothing that would in any capacity represent the sounds. There was nothing before him except for dividers, furniture, and— space. Not a living animal. What at that point caused those sounds? He was posing himself this inquiry when the entryway opened, and Mr. McMahon, trailed by Katherine and the entirety of different young ladies, came into the loft; and, with their entrance, the bizarre sounds without a moment's delay stopped.

"Why, what's wrong, Mr. O'Farrell," the young ladies said, laughingly. "You are just about as white as a sheet and shaking all finished. You haven't seen an apparition, have you?"

"I haven't seen anything," O'Farrell answered, a triviality annoyed at their joy, "however I've heard some somewhat exceptional sounds."

"Exceptional sounds," Katherine giggled. "What in the world do you mean?"

"Exactly what I say," O'Farrell commented. "At the point when I was on the veranda a little while ago, I unmistakably heard the sound of a harp in this room, and instantly a short time later I heard a lady sobbing."

"It probably been somebody outside in the road," Mr. McMahon noticed quickly, simultaneously giving O'Farrell an admonition looks from his dull and entering eyes. "We do incidentally get visits from road artists. I have a remark to you about the English and their reputed new assault on the town," and drawing O'Farrell to the side he murmured to him: "under no circumstances allude to that music once more. It was without a doubt the Banshee, the phantom that my ancestors brought over from Ireland, and it is just heard before some horrible disaster to the family."

The next day Badajoz was raged and entered by the English, and in the wild scenes that followed, scenes in which the tipsy English soldiery got totally out of hands, numerous Spanish—Spanish people—died, just as French, and among the losses were the whole McMahon family.

BANSHEE IN THE OCEANS

Discussing ghost music, there is a far and wide conviction among Celtic races that at whatever point it is heard continuing from the ocean, either demise or some other extraordinary cataclysm is visualized. Such a conviction is exceptionally predominant along the banks of Scotland, Wales, and Cornwall, and Mr. Dyer, in his "Phantom World,", alludes to it in Ireland. "In some cases," he says, "music is heard adrift, and it is trusted in Ireland that, when a companion or relative kicks the bucket, an admonition voice is recognizable." To what degree this music is associated with Banshee hauntings it is, obviously, difficult to say; however, I have known cases in which it has owed its beginning to the Banshee and the Banshee as it were.

During the Civil War in America, for instance, a vehicle of Confederate warriors was making for Charlestown one evening, when a youthful Irish official, who was hanging absurd and looking meditatively into the ocean, was shocked to hear the best hints of music coming from, so it appeared to him, the actual profundities of the blue waters. Figuring he should dream, he called a sibling official to his side and inquired as to whether he could hear anything.

"Indeed," the last reacted, "music, and what is more, singing. It is a lady, and she is singing some delicate and sad air. How the deuce do you represent it?"

"I don't have the foggiest idea," the youthful Irishman answered, "except if it is the Banshee, and it sounds like the depiction of it that my mom used to give me. I just expected it doesn't foresee the demise of any of my close to family members."

It didn't do that, however strangely, and obscure to him at that point, a namesake of his, whom he thusly found was a subsequent cousin, stood not ten yards from him at the exact instant he was tuning in to the music and was killed in real life in a fight from Charlestown on the next day.

An account of a comparative sort was advised me in Oregon by an old Irish Federal warrior, who was in the transitory utilize of an apple trader at Medford, Jackson County. I don't in any capacity vouch for its reality, yet give it similarly as it was identified with me.

"You inquire as to whether I have at any point run over any phantoms in America. Indeed, I surmise I have, a few, and among others the Banshee. Gracious, indeed, I am Irish, even though I talk with the nasal twang of the normal Yank. Everybody does who has lived in the Eastern States for any time allotment. It's the environment. My name, in any case, is O'Hagan, and I was brought into the world in County Clare; and however, my dad was just a labourer, I'm a darned sight more Irish than a large portion of individuals who have titles and huge bequests in the old country to-day.

"I emigrated from Ireland with my folks, when I was half a month old, and we got comfortable New York, where I was functioning as a doorman on the quays when the Civil War broke out. Like me, most of Irishmen who, as you probably are aware, is consistently all set any place there's the opportunity of doing a touch of battling, I without a moment's delay enrolled in the Marines, for I was enthusiastically attached to the ocean, and at the appointed time of time was moved to a gunboat that watched the Carolina Coast keeping watch for Confederate bar sprinters. All things considered, one evening, not long after I had turned in and was lying in my lounger, attempting to will rest, which was none excessively simple, for one of my mates, an ex-entertainer, was wheezing uproarious enough to wake the entire boat, I abruptly heard a tapping on the window close next to me. 'Hi,' says I to me, 'that is an odd clamour. It can't be the water, nor yet the breeze; perhaps it's a bird, a gull or gooney bird,' and I listened mindfully. The sound went on, yet it had none of that hardness and sharpness about it that is occasioned by a snout, it was gentler and seriously waiting, more like the tapping of fingers. From time to time, it left off, to go on once more, tap, tap, tap, until, finally, it scared me so much that I leapt out of my lounger and had a peep to perceive what it was. To my shock I saw a white face squeezed against the opening, glancing in at me. It was the essence of a lady with raven dark hair that fell in long curls about her neck and shoulders. She had huge brilliant rings in her ears, that shone like anything as the moonbeams got them, as did her teeth which were the loveliest pieces of ivory, I have at any point seen, totally even and without the smallest blemish.

"In any case, it was her eyes that intrigued me most. They were huge, not excessively huge, nonetheless, but rather in the severe extent to the remainder of her face, and to the furthest extent that I could decide in the evening glow, either blue or dark, yet indefinably lovely, and, simultaneously, unbelievably tragic. As I moved closer, she shrank back, and pointed with a white and slim hand at a spot on the ocean, and afterwards, out of nowhere I heard music, the distant sound of a harp, continuing, so it appeared to me, from about the spot she had demonstrated. It was a still evening, and the sounds came to me unmistakably, over the delicate lap, lap of the water against the vessel's side, and the mechanical crush, crunch made by the bows each time they rose and fell, as the boat tenderly furrowed her direction onwards.

I was so aiming at listening that I very failed to remember the figure of the lady with the wonderful face, and when I went to take a gander at her once more, she had gone, and there was nothing before me except for an unending territory of hurling, throwing twilight water. At that point, the music stopped, as well, and everything was still again, wondrously still, and feeling untouchably dismal and forlorn—for I had taken an extraordinary extravagant to that lady's face, the solitary what you may term truly stunning lady's face that had at any point looked mercifully on me—I got back again into my lounger and was before long sleeping soundly. On my contacting at the port, the principal letter I got from home educated me regarding the passing of my dad, who had kicked the bucket that very evening and pretty much a similar time I had seen that pixie vision and heard that pixie music.

"At the point when I educated my mom regarding it, some lengthy timespan thereafter, she said it was the Banshee, and that it had frequented the O'Hagan family for a great many years."

This, as I have effectively said, is simply a trooper's story, unsubstantiated by any other person's proof, and, obviously, not up to the norm of S.P.R. authority. However, I accept, it was identified with me in amazing earnestness, and the storyteller had nothing whatever to acquire through making it up. I didn't considerably offer him a bite of tobacco, for at that point I was very almost, if not, undoubtedly, very however hard up as he seemed to be himself.

Also, presently, before I finish through and through with Banshee hauntings that are related to war, I believe I should allude to an assertion in Mr. Michael's book, "Irish Wonders," such that when the Duke of Wellington passed on, the Banshee was heard moaning round the place of his predecessors. This proclamation doesn't, as I would see it, bear examination. I'm very prepared to give that some sort of spectre—maybe a family apparition he had acquired from one or other of his Anglo-Irish heritage—was heard mourning external the space being referred to; yet as the family to whom the Duke had a place couldn't be supposed to be of anything moving toward antiquated Irish extraction, I can't imagine it conceivable that the aggravations experienced were in any capacity because of the certified Banshee.

To return to the ocean, and Banshee frequenting. On the bank of Donegal there is an estuary called "The Rosses," and this at one at once to be spooky by a few sorts of apparitions, including the Banshee, which was accounted for to have shown itself on a lot of events.

Under the heading of "An Irish Water-beast," Bourke, in his "Accounts of the Aristocracy" (I. 329), relates the accompanying instance of a spooky occurring there, which, albeit not because of a Banshee, is so normal for Irish extraordinary marvels that I can't forgo citing it.

In the harvest time of 1777 the Rev. James Crawford, minister of the area of Kilian, County Lei trim, was riding a horse with his sister-in-law, Miss Hannah Wilson, on a pillion behind him, along the street prompting "The

Rosses," and, on arriving at the estuary, he without a moment's delay continued to cross it. After they had gone some distance, Miss Wilson, seeing that the water contacted the seat laps, turned out to be frightened to the point that she shouted out and bethought Mr. Crawford to turn the pony adjust and return to land as fast as could be expected.

"I don't think there can be a risk," Mr. Crawford replied, "for I see a horseman crossing the portage not twenty yards before us."

To this Miss Wilson, who additionally saw the horseman, answered: "You would be wise to hail him and ask the profundity of the mediating water."

Mr. Crawford without a moment's delay did as such, whereupon the horseman paused and, turning round, uncovered a face twisted by the most terrible smile possible, thus unpleasantly white and insidious that the unfortunate minister immediately beat a retreat, and made no endeavour to check the distraught scramble of his terrified horse till he had left the estuary numerous miles behind him.

On showing up the home he portrayed the occurrence to his significant other and family and accordingly discovered that the estuary was well known to be spooky by a few ghosts, whose mission was perpetually something very similar, either to prognosticate the destruction by suffocating of the individual to whom they showed up, or, in all likelihood to achieve the passing of that individual by drawing them endlessly, until they escaped their profundity, thus died.

One would have believed that Mr. Crawford, after the experience just described, would have given the estuary an exceptionally wide compartment in future; yet nothing of the sort. He again endeavoured to cross the passage of "The Rosses" on 27th September 1777 and was suffocated in the undertaking.

Among many exciting thus (it struck me at that point) real stories advised me in my childhood by a Mrs. Holmes, a notable seller of oranges and chocolate in Bristol, were a few blending records of the Banshee. I was at the time a day kid at Clifton College, a dwelling not exceptionally a long way from the school, and Mrs. Holmes, who used to visit our home each week with her products, took a specific premium in me since I was Irish—one of "the genuine old O'CONNORonnell's." She was a local of Cork, and had, I accept, relocated from that city in the Juno, an old dairy cattle boat, that for over twenty years utilized consistently among Cork and Bristol conveying a modest bunch of travellers, who, for the affordability of the charge, made the best of the rolling and throwing and very restricted space apportioned for their convenience. In later years I frequently headed out to and from Dublin and Bristol in the Argo, the Juno's sister transport, so I talk feelingly and as a matter of fact. In any case, to continue with Mrs. Holmes's Banshee stories.

The one containing a record of a Banshee frequenting on the ocean I will describe in this part, and the other, which has no association with one or the other ocean or waterway, I will manage later on.

Before I start either story, in any case, I might want to say that however Mrs. Holmes talked with a rich brogue and was truly Irish, she utilized hardly any, of those words and articulations that specific teachers of the Dublin Academic School consider indivisible from the discourse of the Irish worker class. I can't, for instance, recollect her steadily saying Masha, or Array, or Oro; and, concerning Erse, I am very sure she didn't have the foggiest idea about an expression of it. However, as I have said, she was Irish, and undeniably more Irish than a significant number of the Gaelic researchers of today who, unendurably glad for their insight into the Celtic tongue, bore one solid by their weak and worthless endeavours to secure something of the genuine Irish mind and acknowledged humour.

Mrs. Holmes didn't frequently talk about her folks; they were, I extravagant, labourers, or, maybe, what we should term "little ranchers," and from what I could accumulate they lived, at one time, in a little town right external Cork; however, Mrs. Holmes was, she advised me, attached to the ocean, and regularly, when a young lady, strolled into Cork and went out sailing with her young companions in Queenstown harbour.

On one event, she and another young lady and two youngsters went for a sail with an old angler they knew, who took them some distance up the coast toward Kinsale. There had been a slight breeze when they began, however, it dropped unexpectedly as they were attaching to return home, and since the sails must be brought down and paddles utilized, both the young fellows elected to push. Their offer is acknowledged by the old angler, they pulled away consistently till they espied an old boat, so battered and eroded as to be minimal more than a simple shell, lying half in and half out of the water in a minuscule bay. At that point, as the climate was flawlessly fine and nobody was in a rush to return home, it was suggested that they pull up to the disaster area and look at it. The old angler challenged, yet he was before long prevailed upon, and the two young fellows and Mrs. Holmes's young lady companion loaded up the old mass, leaving Mrs. Holmes and the old angler in the boat. The shadows from the trees and shakes had effectively shown themselves on the shimmering shingles of the seashore, and a gleam, radiating from the quickly rising moon and bunches of glimmering stars that each second shone forward with expanded brilliancy, appeared each item around them with alarming uniqueness.

Continuously in her component in scenes of this portrayal, Mrs. Holmes was having a ball to the most extreme. Inclining toward the side of the boat and following one hand in the water, she savoured the new night air, aromatic with the fragrance of blossoms and ozone. She could hear her companions talking and snickering as they attempted to consistent themselves on the slanting sheets of the old mass; and as of now, one of them, Jacky, suggested that they ought to dive underneath the deck and investigate the lodges. At that point, their voices continuously developed fainter and fainter, until ultimately completely was still, save for the lapping of the ocean against the sides of the boat, and the delicate weave of the wavelets as they broke on the seashore, and an intermittent far-away barking's of a canine—commotions that in some way or another appear to have a place with summer more than to some other time of the year.

Mrs. Holmes's memory, stirred by these sounds, ventured out back to past seasons, and she was portraying a portion of the old scenes over once more, when at the same time, from the disaster area, from that side of it, so she couldn't help suspecting, that was part of the way submerged, there rang out a progression of the most shocking shouts, very much like the shouts of a lady who had been unexpectedly jumped upon and either wounded or treated in some similarly savage and rough way.

Mrs. Holmes, obviously, on the double thought about her companion, Julia Rooney, and, grasping the boatman by the arm, she shouted:

"The Saints over, it's Julia. They're killing her."

"'Tis no lady, that," the old boatman said dryly. "'Tis the Banshee, and I would not have had this have occurred for the entire favoured world. I wish my mom so sick in bed with the stiffness and cool she got all through her with sitting out on the wet grass the prior night last."

"Are you certain?" Mrs. Holmes murmured, grasping him tighter, while her teeth prattled. "Is it true that you are certain it isn't Julia, and they are not executing her?"

"Sure," answered the boatman, "that is how the Banshee consistently shouts—'tis her, right enough, 'tis no human lady," and like the great Catholic that he was, he crossed himself, and, plunging the paddles tenderly into the water, he started to pull gradually and unobtrusively away.

Before long the shouting stopped, and after a second the three wayfarers came marching on to the deck, giving no indications whatever of caution, and when addressed for whether they had heard anything, laughingly answered in the negative.

"Just," Jacky added wryly, "the kiss Michael Power took from Julia. That was all."

In any case, for Jacky that was not all. At the point when he showed up home, he found that during his nonattendance his mom had kicked the bucket abruptly, and, without a doubt, at the exact second when Mrs. Holmes and the boatman had heard the Banshee.

SUMMARY

The source of the Banshee is very normal contrasted with the stories that encompass her. In bygone eras, during memorial services, a lady would assume the job of 'quicker'. Keeners sang pitiful tunes, called 'coined' – the Irish word for 'crying' – at the graveside. There was acceptable business to be made as a quicker, as families would compensate fairly for a capable one. The most popular ones consistently went to the memorial services of the greatest and most notable individuals and were abundantly pursued, as the more individuals grieving at a memorial service, the more noteworthy the individual was supposed to be. For the most remarkable families, it was a typical conviction that a 'bean Sidhe', or 'pixie lady' would come to sharp at the grave; pixies being more gifted artists than any human. The Irish expression got anglicized to 'Banshee' and over the long run, the tales formed and transformed into what we know today. The way that the keeners were paid in liquor and frequently wound up as older alcoholic ladies that were ousted from towns and towns likewise adds to the fantasy. The initially known put down the account of a Banshee story is Sean McCreath's 'Catherin Catherin', or 'Wins of Turlough'.

Initially, the Banshee seemed to individuals who were going to endure a savage and difficult passing, like homicide. In later stories, she howled outside their entryway around evening time (ordinarily around lush territories nearby) yet was once in a while seen. Critics and pragmatists who guarantee the story to be simply an old spouses' story say that the howls are in reality stable owls or ladies bringing in the evening. On the off chance that you've at any point heard either creature, they do sound astoundingly like a lady shrieking! The Banshee was generally portrayed as revolting older ladies wearing white or dim with long silver hair, and every so often appeared as a crow, stoat, rabbit or weasel – common creatures related with black magic in Ireland.

The Banshee comes in three potential appearances relying upon who you converse with or where the narratives come from. All the more frequently than not she is a squatting witch with a shocking wrinkly face, albeit in different stories she is a wonderful, ethereal young lady or an impressive lady type. In yet more stories she is alluded to as the apparition of a killed lady or a lady who kicked the bucket in labour. The three normal pretences of the Banshee may represent the three parts of the Celtic goddess of war and demise; Badshah, Macha and Morrigan.

In practically all cases, the Banshee has long silver hair that she is now and again seen brushing with a brush. Therefore, a few groups could never get a look overlying on the ground because of a paranoid fear of being removed by pixies. She wears a dark hooded shroud or the white sheet or grave robe of the dead, and her eyes are red from crying. Many accept that she can truly be told to take on any of the above structures and change from one to the next however she sees fit.

Her cry is by all accounts the subject of much discussion; in Leinster, it is supposed to be harsh to such an extent that it breaks the glass. Further north in Tyrone she sounds more like two sheets being struck together, while in Kerry her call is 'low, lovely singing'. Whatever she looks like, everybody concurs that she can be heard from a significant stretch. Some report hearing her sob for a few evenings in succession before a demise happened, while others say they heard her only once, the evening of the passing. Her cry rises and falls and goes on for in any event a couple of moments, differing in force.

There have been asserted occurrences when the Banshee wept for an individual who was in amazing wellbeing, however, was discovered dead inside seven days from some monstrosity mishap. Most of her visits are paid around evening time, with a little barely any occurring around early afternoon. The Banshee was generally thought to have once been a typical lady who delighted throughout everyday life, was staggeringly wonderful and emanated joy, however, some extraordinary distress conquered her eventually in her life and she turned into a rundown elderly person. She was extremely tired of humans and would vanish whenever there's any hint of any human action. Indeed, she didn't appear to appreciate the organization of anybody, mortal or not, and went as a singular pixie.

At the point when the Banshee moved from one spot to another, witnesses have heard a rippling sound like birds flying. At the point when she vanished, all that would be given up was a haze of fog. There are a few implied 'Banshee Chairs' around Ireland; wedge moulded rocks where she would sit and sob for general disasters if there was no demise to be taken care of that is! At the point when a family emigrated, allegedly the

Banshee would follow, or if she didn't, she would remain at the family's seat and mourn their leaving there.

REFERENCES

Following are the references that were used and just consulted to make this book a success, we are thankful for your cooperation towards our book.

- https://www.yourdictionary.com/banshee Basics and meanings of Banshees from yourdictionary.com.

- https://en.wikipedia.org/wiki/Banshee The sights and main information gathered and rephrased from Wikipedia.org.

- https://www.britannica.com/topic/banshee Formal knowledge regarding banshees gathered from Britannica.org to make the readers more aware of the happening and beings of the banshees.

- https://www.claddaghdesign.com/history/irelands-best-known-spirit-the-banshee/ The signs and concerns about the banshees are formulated from claddaghdesign.com to make the readers aware of the regions and occurring's of Banshees.

- https://www.yourirish.com/folklore/banshees-in-ireland Few insights of the story are formed from this website and are rephrased.

The above references are just for knowledge for the readers, the contents are completely made in our own words and it has complete rights of the honour and the author of the book.

We hope you enjoy reading our book. CHEERS AND THANKS.